C000246454

PLEASURE AND PERIL IN SNOWDONIA

St Mary and St Bodfan Church, Llanaber

Pleasure and Peril in Snowdonia

Barmouth
and the 1894 Boating Tragedy

Paula Burnett

First published in 2021

© text and images listed below: Paula Burnett

© Gwasg Carreg Gwalch 2021

All rights reserved. No part of this publication
may be reproduced, stored in a retrieval system,
or transmitted in any form or by any means, electronic,
electrostatic, magnetic tape, mechanical, photocopying,
recording, or otherwise, without prior permission
of the authors of the works herein.

ISBN: 978-1-84524-308-1

Cover design: Eleri Owen

Published by Gwasg Carreg Gwalch,
12 Iard yr Orsaf, Llanrwst, Wales LL26 0EH
tel: 01492 642031
email: books@carreg-gwalch.cymru
website: www.carreg-gwalch.cymru

Picture acknowledgements: Gail Hall, 74.1; National Archive, 19;
National Library of Wales, 30; Nefyn.com, 57; Bernard O'Connor, 111;
Press, i[?], 5.1&2, 71, 74.2, 77.1&2, 78; Hugh Griffith Roberts, 12, 55, 68, 81.1, 84.

Author's photographs: pages 2, 10, 29, 59, 66, 69.1, 80, 81.2, 82.1&2, 87, 91.1&2,
93.1&2, 95, 98.1&2, 99, 101.

Author's collection: pages 18, 21, 58, 64, 65, 67.1&2, 69.2, 70, 73, 76, 82.1&2, 89.1.

Winter sunshine on Cader Idris and Barmouth bridge

Summer mist in the estuary

A Foreword

This is a detailed, humane and intimate historical detective account, taking a Victorian boating tragedy on the Mawddach river in Meirionnydd, and piecing together the bittersweet human stories of the people who lost their lives, their fellow-travellers and the Barmouth community that depended on tourism for a living. It is a story of the confidence of youth and the deference of local boatmen, and how they fell fatally foul of the hazards of nature. It's a story of media prurience and reputational damage. Fundamentally, though, it's a morality tale about the fragility of precious life, and how good intentions can lead to fatal results.

Liz Saville Roberts MP

Safety in the Mountains

The mountains of Eryri are a wonderful and diverse collection of gems, accessible to most people and depending on **experience** and **ability**, they can be enjoyed in all weathers and seasons. Despite their beguiling and often welcoming appearance, the mountains can, and do, bite back. The central and southern mountains of Eryri are quieter and less frequented than their northern neighbours and therefore have a wilder and more remote feel. That is their charm!

The three Mountain Rescue Teams that cover the area – Aberglaslyn, South Snowdonia and Aberdyfi are frequently called out to assist walkers in distress, often at quite unsociable hours. These incidents vary considerably in their nature – some are genuine and unfortunate accidents but an increasing number are quite avoidable and if only a little time had been spent in preparation and planning, a much better day would have been had by all and the teams could have enjoyed their supper.

The main safety points to consider are:

1. Plan a route within the ability of **all** the members of the group. Get acquainted with your planned route beforehand from maps/internet/books etc. Remember that the summit is only half way and that most incidents occur on the way down when the party is tired. Pay particular attention to the weather forecast.

2. Wear adequate clothing and footwear for the walk, taking the terrain and weather into account. Take spare clothing, food, drink and adequate lights for everybody. The temperature will probably drop by 1°C with every 150m climbed and the wind will probably strengthen considerably. Find out what time it gets dark – there are no street lights!

3. Make an early start and be prepared to retreat if conditions deteriorate or members of the group are unwilling or unable to continue. There is no shame in turning back. Be competent in the use of a map and compass – don't depend on a mobile phone for maps and lights. They don't like cold and wet. They can, and do fail.

4. Tell a responsible person of your plans for the day – departure point, intended route, time of return etc. so that should things go wrong, the teams will have some idea where to look...

Finally, remember the words of the great Victorian Alpinist, Edward Whymper.

...climb if you will, but remember that courage and strength are naught without prudence, and that a momentary negligence may destroy the happiness of a lifetime. Do nothing in haste, look to each step, and from the beginning think what may be the end.

They are as valid today as they were in 1871.

Myfyr Tomos.
SNPA Cadair Idris Warden and Callout Coordinator
for the South Snowdonia Team.

Contents

Introduction

On the south wall of the nave of Barmouth's ancient parish church at Llanaber is a brass plaque lettered in black and red. It commemorates the ten young people who lost their lives in the Mawddach[1] estuary on what should have been a pleasant summer holiday excursion. Many visitors to the beautiful thirteenth-century church – like an upturned boat on the shore, beached safely above the waves – will have seen the memorial, but few know the story of who those people were, and what happened on 1 August 1894. It seems to have been largely forgotten, yet it is an absorbing story, and one still of significant relevance today.

It offers an illuminating insight into the hopes and achievements of late nineteenth-century society and the optimism and talents of some ordinary young people, but above all it demonstrates the power of responsibility – how seemingly small-scale, innocuous decisions and actions taken or not taken can combine with chance, with forces beyond our control, to produce catastrophic results. In doing so it also reminds us that the heroism of individuals' responses is of little comfort or utility once a disastrous chain of events is set in motion. It is above all a very human story. It examines not only the question of individual responsibility, but also that of public bodies tasked with keeping people safe while promoting healthy activities and defending individual liberties.

The first part of this book begins with the victims themselves, who they were, where they came from, why they were in Barmouth (in Welsh Abermaw or Bermo). As young but serious-minded members of the National Home Reading

Memorial plaque on south interior wall of Llanaber church

Union they were on an educational as well as recreational holiday, a fact that is reflected in the inclusion of poems they might have known. The second part then presents an account of the unfolding disaster as reported in newspapers across the country, from eye-witness accounts and from evidence given to the coroner just a few hours after the catastrophic events. The third part enables the fateful excursion up the estuary on that August evening in 1894 which began so pleasurably, to be brought back to life in our time with illustrations of the scenes involved. In its final part the story returns to the wider context of that night's implications, in parallel with other tragic events, and, while honouring selfless heroism and service, asks what we can usefully learn today from the reasons why, on certain occasions, tragedy has been the sad outcome.

'Health and Safety' is a phrase heard everywhere now and often mocked, seen as thwarting excitement and the pleasures of thrill-seekers. As today's authorities, in Snowdonia as elsewhere, are only too aware, the balance between encouraging activity holidays and keeping people safe, while allowing access to potentially dangerous environments, is not always easy to find. When things go wrong we are all smitten with sadness and regret, and want answers as to why.

Loss has always been painful. Undoubtedly the urge to commemorate the dead is as old as humankind, but perhaps less obviously, remembering such loss can be a stimulus to preserving life in the future. This book begins with a focus on what should have been a health-giving holiday, examines a particular tragedy involving the loss of young and optimistic lives, and ends with a focus on safety.

I

An Evening in August

Barmouth bridge, 1894

An Evening in August

The railway which had arrived in Barmouth in 1867 over the newly built iconic viaduct spanning the estuary, which made the summer influx of holidaymakers from all over the country so easy, was put to a tragic task over the coming days, carrying young people's coffins back to the communities they had come from.

Only one of the victims is buried at Llanaber, the youngest, the seventeen year-old younger sister of a survivor, mourned by her parents and the sister who had been saved.

The report in the *Cheshire Observer* is typical of the news flashed by telegraph all over the country, from Aberdeen to Plymouth, as the scale of the tragedy began to emerge:

> A shocking boating accident occurred on Wednesday night on the River Mawddach, a few miles east of Barmouth. In the afternoon a large number of visitors went up to Penmaenpool in pleasure boats, returning thence about half-past eight. On the way home they encountered a heavy gale, and two of the boats capsized, resulting in the loss of ten lives. Eight bodies have been recovered. The boats which went up the river in the afternoon were three in number, and together they conveyed about 20 visitors, as well as Miss Edwards, a resident of Barmouth. Two of the boats were respectively in charge of William Jones and Lewis Edwards, two of the most experienced seafaring men in Barmouth, and two Oxford oarsmen had charge of the third boat.[2]

No less a person than the Coroner was to assert that 'It is well known that these two boatmen are the most competent men in town.' But boatmen, like everyone else, are not always wise.

In fact only one boat went as far as Penmaenpwll.[3] The two in the charge of local boatmen turned back at Bontddu in deteriorating weather after a visit to the Clogau gold mine. But these were no ordinary holidaymakers. The two Oxford oarsmen, William Paton and Percival[4] Gray, were the organisers and leaders of a group holiday for sixty members of the National Home Reading Union, founded just a few years earlier by Paton's father to encourage an ongoing interest in books and self-education in particular in young people. This was Victorian idealism and faith in education at its best, and the young holidaymakers who gathered on the quay that evening were serious-minded book-lovers, mostly nonconformists, intent on self-improvement as well as having an innocent good time.

Described as 'well-known Oxford rowers,'[5] Paton and Gray took the six young women in their boat further upriver, for tea at the George III inn by the tollbridge at Penmaenpwll. Boatman William Jones, who was in charge of one of the other boats, told the inquest that 'Mr. Paton refused a boatman before starting out.'[6] That refusal is a poignant example of the confidence – the over-confidence – of youth, particularly where young men intend to demonstrate their athletic prowess to a boatload of young women. Class was also at play here. Paton and Gray were university-educated men used to being in charge. William Jones could have refused them the use of his boat the "Margaret" – he was already going out with the "Jane" – but a boatman would have been unlikely to challenge such men, and in any case it would have meant forfeiting the hire fee.

With hindsight the decisions on that quay in weather which was already turbulent enough to deter other possible trippers could – should – have been different. Only the boatmen had the experience to understand fully what the risks might be. They knew the dangers of tide and wind in the estuary, and the speed with which weather could deteriorate. They also knew that navigating as darkness fell was particularly difficult and dangerous. Of the eight in William Paton's boat only one was to come home alive. The boat captained by William Jones also capsized on its return from Bontddu and, despite his best efforts which saved three lives, a further three were drowned.[7] Only Lewis Edwards was to keep his boat afloat and to return all his passengers home. Ten lives in all were lost.

A passenger in Lewis Edwards' boat, Charles Edward Harrison of Derby, said that 'another boatman had intimated to him before starting that it was rather rough, and advised him to take a boatman.'[8] A local Talsarnau man, R. Jones Morris, recorded the weather in his diary, neatly, in ink and in English, as he did every day. For Wednesday 1 August he wrote 'Gusty – Showery... Fair,' then noted that he had mown some hay. Next day he took the train to Barmouth, and set down simply, '10 visitors were drowned at B'mouth last evening.' Nothing more.[9] Since there was a new moon on 1 August 1894, spring tides were not a factor in the tragedy that was to unfold on the river that evening, though the wind certainly was. The key may be in the word 'Gusty.'[10]

At the inquest it was asserted by a spokesman for the Home Reading Union that Paton and Gray had lost their lives trying to save others, as both were good swimmers. That Percival Gray and William Paton were fine young men has never been disputed. They, in particular, were portrayed as the heroes of the hour who gave their lives in attempting to save others. But it emerges from a close study of the available accounts of the tragedy that unfolded that theirs was not the only heroic response to the dire events. As one news report put it, 'I do not remember a disaster in which so much noble unselfishness was testified to.'[11] Nonetheless, sadly, as organisers they, and others, made some bad decisions on that August evening.

The story of the events and of the people involved is still moving, a gripping drama with a tragic outcome. It is also a window onto late Victorian society with all its hopes and fears, horrors and happiness. The people, mainly young, who gathered on Barmouth's harbour wall on that August evening in 1894 with a view to a boating excursion, in the particularities of their lives give us a potent glimpse of the whole country near the end of that remarkable century. The people who died were of course unique, and uniquely precious to their respective families, but we can also see in them the era and its energy, its forward impetus which for those ten was so suddenly cut short. It is painful to reflect how readily that outcome might have been avoided.

Perhaps some of those book-loving visitors would have known Thomas Love Peacock's lines from 'The Song of the Four Winds:'

Wind from the west: the mighty wave
Of ocean bounds o'er rock and sand;
The foaming surges roar and rave
Against the bulwarks of the land:
When waves are rough, and winds are high,
Good is the land that's high and dry.

Wind from the west: the storm-clouds rise;
The breakers rave, the whirl-blasts roar,
The mingled rage of seas and skies
Bursts on the low and lonely shore:
When safety's far, and danger nigh,
Swift feet the readiest aid supply.[12]

The National Home Reading Union

First, what was the National Home Reading Union and who were its members? It had been founded just five years earlier by William's father, the Rev. Dr. John Brown Paton of Nottingham, a prominent Scottish-born theologian, Congregationalist, and graduate of London University (perhaps from its extension programme), to encourage the use of books among those who might otherwise not read or continue with reading outside formal education, such as young people whose schooling was finishing, workers without a family tradition of reading, and those who enjoyed reading but lacked confidence in choosing books.

The founders were firm in their intention for it to be non-denominational, though they themselves were nonconformists and the scheme caught on particularly in nonconformist communities. They also wanted it to appeal across classes, but the modest membership fees and the cost of buying books – although they tried to make special editions available – tended to exclude the bulk of the labouring classes who had no money to spare. The scheme was not about religious or morally improving texts, though it was certainly concerned to direct readers away from trivial and possibly 'dangerous' books and towards those regarded as of intellectual and aesthetic value. The idea was that the organisation would recommend titles in all sorts of fields – literature, history, science, philosophy – for local groups to read together, with regular meetings to discuss their responses and explore the texts further. It was to be something like a modern book club, with the social side later expanded to include not just monthly tea and discussion sessions but a reading holiday in an area where activities such as walks in beautiful scenery would be part of the programme, introduced by local people with knowledge of the places of historic or scenic interest. The rhetoric with which the scheme had been founded had an affinity from the first with healthy outdoor pursuits. Its objective was, said John Paton, to disseminate 'the highlands of our noble literature where blows the free air of heaven to refresh and inspire the mind.'[13] By 1894 it had attracted some 700 members.[14]

The first Home Reading Union holiday had been in the

John Brown Paton (1830-1911), portrait by John Arnesby Brown, 1899

Lake District the year before. For a month or six weeks over the summer different groups of members would arrive for a week's activities. In 1894 Barmouth was chosen. The success of the NHRU in spreading and attracting members in so few years is evident in that sixty, mainly young, people from different parts of the country had arrived there by train on the last Saturday in July for a week of shared reading, discussion and excursions. Well-known local nonconformist ministers, the Revs. J. Gwynoro Davies and Zechariah Mather,[15] were on hand to introduce places of local interest to the members. Houses had been booked in Barmouth for their board and lodging. Many of those who died were staying at Hendre Villas,[16] a substantial stone-built mansion in Epworth Terrace by what is now the park.

Since all the people on the Wednesday evening's boat trip appear to have been nonconformists – as the assertion that they were all teetotal suggests – it may be that as well as being housed together they tended also to go about as a group. The fact that a photograph was commissioned from a local photographer, Henry Martyn Appleyard, which shows

Hendre Villas are on the right[17]

a group of twenty sitting on a grassy bank, presumably on a walking excursion given the number of walking sticks in evidence, supports this hypothesis, as it was later claimed to have been a photograph of the fateful boat party.

The photographer in the following November even took the trouble to register his copyright in it, under the title 'Photograph of group containing party who met with fatal boating accident in Barmouth Aug 1 1894.'[18]

There is no proof as to whether these were the very individuals who took to boats on the evening of 1 August rather than other members of the National Home Reading Union visiting Barmouth that week, but it is certainly possible, and plausible.

Since William Paton was leader of the group he is likely to be in the photograph. Described as of athletic proportions and over six feet tall, and as offering his hat to bail out the boat, he may be the bearded man on the left with a conspicuous hat and the strap of some sort of bag or binoculars over his shoulder, who does bear some resemblance to John Brown Paton, the father. Could Percival

Gray, the other leader, be the younger man in a sporting cap behind him? Both are smiling in a slightly proprietorial way, whereas most of the other men in the photograph are quite straight-faced as was the convention of the time. Two pairs of sisters were also in the boating party. Given their sisterly resemblance, the paired young women in the front row could well be those four.

Early press reports were clear on the special responsibilities of William Paton and Percival Gray:

> All the victims appear to have been members of the National Home Reading Union, and their visit to Barmouth was in connection with one of the holidays organised by the Union, under the direction of Mr. Grey and Mr. Paton, two of the local secretaries.[19]

Percival Gray was one of the secretaries of the Union's London branch, and William Paton, the founder's son, was secretary of its excursion section.[20]

The group of people who gathered on the quay that summer evening were a remarkable symbol of the changes ushered in during the Victorian era. Led by the two university men were young, book-loving people from modest backgrounds all over the country, particularly the industrial north. Their parents had probably not had much education, but for the children there were different opportunities.

Schooling was now available to all. In particular the respect for learning, for the book, and above all for the Bible, typical of nonconformist communities, was producing at this late stage of the nineteenth century a remarkable flowering of intellectual interests and pursuits, often in grim industrial areas which might to a casual observer have been the last place it would have been expected. Its effect in particular on the hitherto narrowly circumscribed lives of so many young women, like those lost to the Mawddach, must have been revolutionary.

We cannot know what the earlier part of the day had

involved in the way of talks and discussions about books, or whether the exchange of ideas continued as the passengers were rowed up the Mawddach, but its beauties were no doubt not lost on those readers who had sampled the poetry of the era and become attuned to its romantic appreciation of the picturesque.

'View between Barmouth & Dolgelley,' 1813, published by E. Williams, London

To Wordsworth the estuary was 'sublime,' and when Ruskin, the famous art critic, arrived he was so ecstatic about what he saw that he got down from his carriage and walked the last few miles to Barmouth to take it all in. Those cultural pundits who had been central to the wider promotion of the beauties of the Lake District had helped to bring North Wales and in particular the Mawddach equally before the imagination of the nation, and to encourage visits to the area to admire it in person. The last part of the rail journey to Barmouth across the estuary bridge must have been accompanied by many oohs and aahs at the unarguably beautiful view upriver.

The Lives Lost

Percival Gray was twenty-one, an undergraduate at New College, Oxford, and an alumnus of Rugby School.[21] As the second son of Dr Edward Gray, a well-to-do physician of Beaumont Street, 'well-known and highly respected,' he was an Oxford man through and through,[22] and was engaged to the daughter of another Oxford medical man.[23] The inquest heard that he was 'a strong oarsman, being a member of an Oxford University eight.'[24] After graduating he planned to become a clergyman in a poor district of London.

The other rower of the one boat that went as far as Penmaenpwll was William P. Paton, born in 1867, a son of the Rev. Dr. John Paton of Nottingham, founder of the National Home Reading Union, and Principal of the Congregational College there, which was renamed Paton Congregational College in the 1920s and is now Paton House, part of Nottingham University.[25]

William, it was widely reported, was six feet tall and 'a splendid all-round athlete. He was about twenty-seven years of age, and took a prominent part in church and social work.'[26] His grandparents had moved from Scotland to Liverpool, where William worked for his uncle Andrew, a cotton merchant. The reaction of other cotton brokers to the news of his death was effusive:

> The talk was that Mr Paton was a general favourite; that his high-toned example as a man of business was a valued influence for good; that he was as merry and cheerful as he was honest and straightforward; that he was as greatly respected out of the market as in it; that his presence wherever he went was like a ray of sunshine; that his literary and intellectual attainments were of a high order; that he delighted in going about doing good... [27]

William lived with a brother[28] at West Kirby on the Wirral, where 'he was, if possible, even more popular than in Liverpool... His gentle and winsome ways and habitual kindness attached him at once to all with whom he came in contact.' He had been

> instrumental in the formation of the Boys' Club, of which he was the life and soul. He was also on the committee of the Literary Society, and took an active interest in the debates, which were always brightened by his ready speech and strong sense of humour. He was a keen athlete, and was on the committee of the Lingdale Tennis Club.... Actively interested in social work, he was a leading supporter of the Sunday Breakfast Mission... and frequently took large parties of poor children to New Brighton[29] for a "treat" at his own expense.

A strong contingent of mourners from the Liverpool area attended the funeral in Nottingham at which his father officiated. Later in August it was announced that his parents had donated a thousand pounds to the West Kirby Convalescent Home for children in his memory.[30]

William Paton and Percival Gray had both been raised in big families, in prosperous upper middle-class homes with several servants to attend to their needs, including nursemaids when they were little (the Grays had a pageboy and a 'schoolroommaid' in 1891, while the Patons, with the youngest son now at Oxford, had a Swiss nurse, a cook and housemaid), but many of the others in their group who set out on that fateful trip were from very different backgrounds.

Taken together they afford a glimpse of the social range of Barmouth's visitors in the eighteen-nineties, and of the wider Britain from which they came. The industrial towns of the north of England were home to most of the visitors on this Barmouth holiday.

The upward mobility which the Victorian age offered to families in all walks of life is very evident from their stories, as many ordinary working people prospered and raised the next generation to jobs where literacy and education counted for something.

Three of those who lost their lives were young women from Durham who had come down by train on the Saturday. Two were sisters, Louisa Dorothy and Margaret Ella Golightly, known as Louie and Ella. They were daughters of a grocer, William R. Golightly, who had begun as a shop assistant but set up his own business. In 1871 he was living amongst coalminers with his then family of seven, Louisa being the fourth daughter. After two sons (one of whom was to die aged thirteen) Margaret was the last child. By 1881 William had progressed to being commercial manager to a yeast importer. After he died in 1888 his widow lived in the city centre with her unmarried daughters 'on own means.' She had a son who was a chemist, one daughter who had been a school teacher, while another had been a milliner. Margaret by 1891 was a teacher's assistant. The family had done well.

A local paper reported both sisters to be 'about 20 years of age,' though Louisa was in fact 32 and Margaret 22 when they died. Louisa, it said, 'was engaged as a designer at Messrs Henderson's carpet factory,[31] at Durham, and had shown much skill in her profession' – a reminder of how women were becoming increasingly important in the workplace by the last decade of the century, and of how the genteel accomplishments seen traditionally as suitable for young ladies, such as a talent for art, were in some cases leading those who did not come from gentrified backgrounds to highly skilled creative jobs in industry. It was a self-improvement path particularly associated with serious-minded nonconformist communities. The report went on: 'Both young ladies were prominently identified with the Wesleyan Methodist connexion, of which body the late Mr Golightly was for many years a much respected lay preacher. The Misses Golightly and other members of the family have ever evinced the greatest interest in everything pertaining to Wesleyan Methodism, and especially in connection with the Durham (Gilesgate) Chapel.'[32]

The sisters' friend was also a Wesleyan and of similar background. She was Sarah Sheldon Greenwell, daughter of 'a grocer and draper of Sherburn Hill near Durham, and a niece of Mr Thomas Greenwell, worsted merchant, of Silver Street, Durham.'[33] Her name was initially reported as Dora (the name of her little sister), but the memorial plaque at Llanaber has the name Sadie italicised in brackets between her first names and surname, so it seems this was how she was known. She was the eldest child of the family and by sixteen had left school. She was not down as having a job but probably helped in the family shop.

At 19 Front Street, Sherburn Village, now a newsagent's, it was in a coalmining area, sandwiched between two public houses, no doubt a stimulating location for a family raising their children to be aware of the evils of drink.

Both Durham families seem to have been typical of nonconformist communities in industrial cities up and down the land. The young women were from eminently respectable families of humble origins, who had made good by dint of hard work and modest living, sufficiently to send their book-loving daughters on an intellectually 'improving' study holiday with like-minded people. Sarah, or Sadie, was just twenty when she set off with her friends for Barmouth.

Herbert Woodworth was also from the industrial north, but from the other side of the Pennines. He was born in 1867 in Salford where his father was a railway porter.

The family moved to Ardwick in south Manchester, the father progressing to 'Carrier' and in 1891 to 'Master Porter.' By this time, however, his three sons were all clerks, pen-pushers rather than labourers like their father.

Herbert, the eldest, was twenty-six when he went to join the Home Reading Union holiday. The report of his death in the local paper said that he was

well known in the neighbourhood of Ardwick. From a very early age he had been connected with the London Road Wesleyan Sunday School, first as a scholar, and then filling the post of teacher, which position he occupied at the time of his death. He had rendered splendid service to the temperance cause, having acted in the capacity of secretary to the Band of Hope at the school. He was one of the original promoters of the Young People's Society of Christian Endeavour at Grosvenor-street, having discharged the duties of correspondence secretary for the past eighteen months. Mr. Woodworth leaves a wide circle of friends, who will deeply regret that a life so full of promise and usefulness should have been cut off at so early an age.

At his funeral 'About 200 of the officers, teachers, and scholars of the London-road Wesleyan Sunday School preceded the hearse to the Grosvenor-street Wesleyan Chapel, where a service was held....' Councillor McDougal, Herbert's employer, sent a wreath.[34] Another newspaper adds, 'He was also a member of the chapel choir.'[35]

The textile industries of the north were the world into which Alice Ann Mallison[36] was born. Her father John was a cotton warp salesman, like his father before him, but he moved from Bolton in Lancashire to Yorkshire, to Manningham in Bradford, where his younger children, Alice Ann and Samuel were born.

By 1881 the family were moving into new realms. The father was 'for a considerable number of years a well-known figure on the Bradford Exchange.'[37]

His eldest daughter was a music teacher aged thirty-two, his next daughter was a weaver, his son a silk dyer, and Alice Ann at seventeen was a teacher. By 1894 she was an elementary teacher of thirty, unmarried, with a taste for books, living with her frail, widowed mother, to whom fate was not kind: 'Miss Mallison's mother, strange to say, received on Thursday morning prior to the news from Barmouth a telegram from Bolton Station that a sister had died there. Mrs. Mallison thus in one day lost a sister and daughter.'[38]

There was another victim from Yorkshire. Marie Reid's father James had been a cabinet maker living in Cemetery Road, Holbeck, Leeds. By 1881 there were five children, Marie being the middle sister of the youngest three, all girls.[39] There were two Reid sisters on the boat trip. Early reports of those drowned included 'Miss Maud Read,'[40] but Maud survived, just, and it was her sister Marie, two years younger, who although she was rescued, could not be revived. The Leeds press reported that she was the niece of Mr. Reid of Park-row, and 'as is perhaps not surprising, was unable to swim.'[41] Marie was still only seventeen, the youngest victim of the tragedy.

Another of those who drowned, whose body was the last to be recovered, was John William Newman, a solicitor's clerk from Dunmow, a small town in rural Essex.[42] His body was found three days after the accident, having been carried upriver by the tide. The location was reported as near Dolgellau – the river is tidal as far as Llanelltyd only – and his body was taken to Dolgellau Workhouse where the inquest was re-opened.

This was a tragic irony as he had grown up at the Dunmow Workhouse, where his father was porter and his mother a laundress. They became so much an institution there themselves that they named a son born in 1880 Harry Porter Newman, and when the father died in 1921 the local press reported that he had been porter at the Union-house (as by then it was more decorously known) for over forty years.

By 1891 his son John was down as a solicitor's clerk, lodging with a local official to the Board of Guardians who had formal responsibility for the workhouse, with the resonant job title of 'Relieving Officer, Registrar of Births and Deaths, and Collector to the Guardians.'

Like the others, John Newman was progressing beyond the social level of his parents. Although only twenty-one when he died, he had worked in the solicitor's office for seven years, and his colleagues, including one of the firm's principals, turned out *en masse* for his funeral. As a member of the volunteer reserve with the 2nd Essex Regiment he was given full military honours. Sixty soldiers including a firing party, the town's brass band – which played *Adeste Fideles* ('O come all ye faithful') in slow time – and a great crowd accompanied his coffin through a Dunmow in mourning, all its businesses shut and blinds down. Fellow members of the Ancient Order of Foresters (a friendly society designed to support members through hard times) carried his coffin into the church past the military guard of honour with arms reversed. It was an event covered in poignant detail in the local press.

John had just spent two days at the volunteers' camp before returning home and setting off on his bicycle to catch an early train to London. There he was to meet his childhood friend and former colleague Frederick Pryor who had arranged the holiday,[43] before they travelled on together to Wales. Sadly, just days after receiving a postcard written by their son on top of Snowdon, his parents were burying him next to his brother who had died only a few months earlier at the age of nineteen: 'Mr. and Mrs. Newman, for whom much sympathy is expressed, are overwhelmed with grief. The poor young man was liked by everybody who knew him. He could swim, and it is believed that he lost his life in trying to save a young lady.'[44] The inquest was to hear testimony of valiant efforts to save the two Reid sisters by the two young men from the boat who survived so this seems likely to be true.

The body of Edith Sara Moore of Harrow was evidently never recovered as her death was not registered. It was probably carried out to sea. The last person to see her alive, Ethel Packer, thought that she owed her her life – that Edith deliberately let go of the plank both were holding on to in the water as it could only support one. She too was from a family connected with the textile industry. Her Devon-born father had lived in Tunbridge, Kent, where Edith was born, but by the time she was four he had moved the family to

Hammersmith where he set up shop as a linen draper. By 1891 when he was in his fifties, he is described as a woollen merchant, living in Rockwood Villa, Station Grove, Harrow, in north London. He had evidently prospered.

Edith was now a book-loving art student[45] living at home. She was twenty-eight when she travelled to Barmouth for the Home Reading Union holiday. Poignantly, she was described joining the boating party by one of their group who chose to stay behind:

> One young lady, Miss Edith Moore, of Harrow, who was among the drowned, and whose body has not yet been recovered, stepped into one of the boats at the last moment, just as it was leaving the Quay, at the same time making a jesting remark to some of her companions respecting the duration of the sail.[46]

Ynys Enlli, Bardsey Island, from Barmouth

II

The Unfolding of a Tragedy

Charles James Lewis, 'Unloading Nets, Barmouth,' c.1880

In the middle of the week's holiday for the National Home Reading Union members, on Wednesday 1 August, a day when an official excursion had not been arranged, a plan emerged to round off the day's activities with an evening river trip. It emerged at the inquest that several of the party had been boating on previous evenings since their arrival in Barmouth. The ten for whom it was to be a voyage of no return were among the twenty-one who decided to set off. A larger group had gathered on the quay but many decided not to embark when they saw the turbulence of the weather.

Three rowing boats were hired from the harbour, two with a boatman in charge, the group having been advised to take boatmen with them because of the rough conditions. William Jones captained his boat the "Jane" with seven passengers, and Lewis Edwards had six in the "Rosa." On the return journey a local woman who had gone out with William Jones joined Lewis Edwards' boat instead. It proved to be a lucky move. The last to leave Barmouth harbour was rowed by the two organisers, the 'Oxford oarsmen' who were confident they did not need a local boatman. The "Margaret" set off with eight on board, the two rowers and six women. The three boats left harbour in the early evening, but already warning bells should have been heard. One boatman said he had not been told how far they were planning to go.

One of the Reading Union group who had intended to go decided against it when he saw the state of the wind and water. A middle-aged Sheffield draper, Mathias Hubbard gave evidence at the inquest:

> Mr. Hubbert [sic], a member of the party, stated that he saw the boats start. They did not seem to be overladen. He did not go in the boat because he perceived the danger, the wind being very high. He denied that the party went out against the will of the boatmen.[1]

One who did go, Charles Edward Harrison of Derby, testified that 'another boatman had intimated to him before starting that it was rather rough, and advised him to take a boatman.'[2]

All the reports stress that the two boatmen who went with the party were among the most experienced in Barmouth. Both were Barmouth born. In the 1891 census Lewis Edwards appears as a fifty-two year-old mariner living near the station with his family. William Jones, fifty-five, is down as Master Mariner, living with his wife and a servant in Victoria Place, next to Hendre Villas where those who drowned had been staying.[3] Robert Morris, one of several boatman who helped recover the bodies as that dreadful night wore on, and who gave evidence at the inquest, was a younger man, about thirty, the son of a coal merchant born in Bontddu, with an elder brother who was a boat builder. Maritime activities were a key part of Barmouth life at this date, as throughout its history.

Mathias Hubbard contacted his local press when he went home to put on record his perspective on the unfolding tragedy in Barmouth a few days earlier (including the poignant account of Edith Moore). He adopted a defensive tone:

> Mr. Hubbard explained that he had sought an interview because the visitors, as a party, felt that in consequence of the varied reports it had been sought to cast upon them the reflection that they were to blame for the accident – an impression he wished to destroy. The accident, as stated, occurred on Wednesday night. Early in the morning of the day the party, numbering 60 in all, decided to go up the river Mawddach as far as Penmaenpool, but later on the wind arose, and they began to be doubtful as to the advisability of making the trip. All the party, therefore, met on the Quay, and inquired of the boatman what the night was going to be like. Mr. Hubbard says the majority of the boatmen replied they could take the party up the river and bring them back quite safely, though one boatman told Mr. Hubbard personally he would not take him for £100.

Another said if the party left at six o'clock in the evening they could get back by 9.30. The boatmen kept pressing the visitors to make the journey, and ultimately about 20 of them agreed to go, the remainder being afraid. Mr. Hubbard was very emphatic in stating that the 20 visitors were persuaded into going by the boatmen's assertions that there was no danger. The party left the Quay at Barmouth about 6.45 in the evening in three boats....

The time was clearly a factor. Although it stays light until quite late in the evening in the summer on the western coast, even past nine o'clock if the sky is clear, such a late start for such an extensive trip was already quite risky. Penmaenpwll is about eight miles upriver from Barmouth, a substantial distance in any conditions. Given the state of the tide and the wind, both of which would have made the return journey much harder, although at other times with the flow of the river it might have been easier, it is remarkable that experienced boatmen were willing to contemplate it – and even to countenance a trip to the Bontddu goldmine before returning. The risk of darkness falling before the boats had returned to harbour was only too real.

The special supplement published in the *Cambrian News* on 10 August described the river:

The river is navigable for small craft to the bridge at Penmaenpool which is about eight miles from Barmouth, and Penmaenpool, having hotel accommodation, is the terminus for a small steam launch which daily plies,[4] and of boating trips generally. The river is about a mile wide near its confluence with the sea, but between three and four miles up from the railway bridge it is narrowed to a few hundred yards by comparatively high headlands which form a sort of gap. With a skilled boatman in charge there is no danger on ordinary occasions. In consequence of the shifting channels and the shallows, however, it is never advisable for amateurs in boating to go up the river; and it is particularly dangerous when the tide is running strongly out against a south-westerly wind as was the case on Wednesday evening. On such occasions the water in the gap is thrown up into waves, which cannot be less than dangerous to river boats however skilfully managed.

Mr Hubbard went on to enlarge on some of the controversial assertions as to the start:

Mr. Hubbard emphatically denies the statement that the visitors pressed the boatmen to take them out, and says the exact opposite was the case.[5] The various boatmen on the quay appealed to the visitors individually to go, and the majority of the men assured them it was safe to make the journey. Unfortunately the secretaries of the Home Reading Union were away, and there was no one to say the journey should not be made.[6]

Clearly the boatmen could, and perhaps should, have refused the hire. Mathias Hubbard's evidence continued:

As the evening wore [on] the wind got higher and the sea rougher, and those of the party who had declined to make the trip became anxious concerning the safety of their friends. It was between 11 and 12 o'clock that they first heard something was wrong. About that time the passengers in the first of the three boats returned in a very exhausted condition. Their story of how their boat had been run ashore four miles from Barmouth, in consequence of the rough water, created a feeling of anxiety for the safety of the occupants of the other two boats, which was intensified by the entire absence of information concerning their whereabouts. The alarm, said Mr. Hubbard, spread.

These were Lewis Edwards' passengers. He had embarked

on the return journey from Bontddu but soon abandoned it, given the state of the wind and water, and turning back to the jetty landed his passengers to make their way back to Barmouth on foot – all except one who was lame, who returned with the boatman. Mathias Hubbard goes on:

An adjournment was made to the Quay in the hope of news, but instead of reassuring tidings, the first thing seen was Miss Reed [Reid], of Leeds, one of the members of the pleasure party, who was lying in the mortuary, surrounded by four doctors, who were trying to restore respiration. Another young lady, named Miss Packer, of Leeds, who had been rescued after prolonged immersion, was in a house on the Quay. Both ladies had been brought in by the boatman of the second boat, and he had left three others at a farmhouse four miles up the river. The party sat up until three o'clock in the morning, in the hope of further news, but none was forthcoming, although between that hour and six o'clock seven bodies were brought in. They were Mr. Percival Gray, 21, Oxford; Mr. W.P. Paton, 33, 7, Long Lane Street, West Kirby, Liverpool; Mr. H. Woodworth, 27, Green Street, Ardwick Green, Manchester; Miss Golightly and Miss Ella Golightly, Lilac House, Durham; Miss Greenwell, Durham; and Miss Mallison, Bradford. These with Miss Reed [Reid], brought in the previous night, Mr. J.W. Newman, Dunmow, Essex, whose body was recovered on Saturday, and Miss Edith Moore, of Harrow, who has not yet been found, made up the total death roll. Naturally enough, such an affair so terrible put an end to all enjoyment.

Medical help was quickly summoned when Lewis Edwards' boat the "Rosa" arrived back, carrying also William Jones and its helpless passengers. Dr Hughes[7] who lived by the harbour and Dr Lloyd[8] who lived further along the High Street did all they could to revive Marie Reid but without result. In fact all of the bodies brought in as the night wore on had clearly been dead for some time. Remarkably it seems Edith Packer who had been so long in the water (an hour it was said) began to recover quite quickly after she was taken to a house on the quay.

The *Cambrian News* painted a vivid picture of the next morning:

> On Thursday morning when the visitors and inhabitants woke they heard with grief and consternation the news of the accident. At once there was a complete cessation of business and pleasure as the news spread from group to group and from house to house, carrying with it sickening wonder as to who the victims were, and what was the exact extent of the loss of life. During the night the bodies had been brought down by the search parties and deposited in the mortuary on the Quay, around which on Thursday morning crowds gathered anxious to learn the particulars of the calamity which had filled the place with its victims.

Inquests began immediately in those days. On 2 August, the day which had dawned with news of the tragedy, the press reported 'The Coroner's inquest will be held this afternoon.'[9]

Telegraph wires hummed with the terrible news:

> The relatives appear to have got their first intimation of the disaster by the accounts in the evening papers [which appeared from lunchtime onwards], and during the inquest on Thursday afternoon telegrams were received by Major Best[10] making anxious enquiries for further particulars of identification. On Thursday relatives of nearly all arrived, and so affecting were the scenes on seeing the dead bodies of their loved ones, that the bystanders were affected to tears.

On the Friday the melancholy journeys home with coffins began at Barmouth's little station. The exception was the body of Marie Reid which was 'privately interred in Llanaber Churchyard on Saturday morning, the Rector of Barmouth officiating, and Mrs Reed, Mr Reed, and Miss Reed attending as chief mourners.' Maud Reid then had to travel home to Leeds with her parents but without her sister.

The inquest opened at the Police Station at 1pm on Thursday before the Coroner, W. R. Davies, and a jury of fourteen. It heard identification evidence and then detailed accounts of what happened. Its proceedings were followed all over the country with extensive reports in the papers, but of course no verbatim account of the testimony exists. Although some reporters were evidently shorthand writers, the news reports are simply versions of the evidence, sometimes confusing and contradictory. The *Cambrian News* supplement claimed superior status in having been allowed to draw on the Coroner's inquest data.

To return to the quayside early on that fateful evening of 1 August, another account gives a rather different perspective. The testimony to the inquest of William Jones, Master Mariner, can perhaps best be relied on, though of course he had his professionalism to defend:

> On Wednesday evening Mr. Paton came to me and said he required two boats to go up the estuary. I replied that it was rather rough and that he would require a boatman to go with him, to which he replied that he was a champion rower of Oxford and quite capable of taking charge of the other boat, and none of the party mentioned anything about it being too rough. I went out in the boat called the Jane. Mr. Paton had the boat called the Margaret. The Jane is registered to carry eight persons and a boatman. I had only seven in it. Edwards was in charge of the third boat. Mr. Paton went as far as Penmaenpool, and Edwards and myself went ashore near the Clogan [Clogau] Mine. There is a landing there.

The inquest was to hear a challenge to this report of William

Paton's remarks: that he had been only asserting the superior competence of Percival Gray. Perhaps both he and later William Jones were guilty of inflating the representation of their own roles. Ethel Packer's evidence, however, was to confirm Paton's own skills in handling the boat. The upriver journey was relatively easy for the rowers with a rising tide and brisk south-westerly wind to help them against the river current. The boat with the two Oxford oarsmen used to competitive rowing made short work of it, and although it had been the last to leave Barmouth harbour it soon caught up with and overtook the other two boats, each with inexperienced rowers alongside the experienced boatmen.

The return journey, however, was a very different matter. The actual course of the river, as against the sands which are exposed at low tide, runs close to the north and south banks at different points along the estuary, and the experienced boatmen would have known where to position their craft to make best progress against a head wind. The two men from Oxford would not have had that knowledge, and were on their own far upriver.

After visiting the Clogau gold mine which is a short walk above Bontddu the passengers returned to the two boatmen. Lewis Edwards takes up the story:

> Yesterday evening I took a boatload of six people up the estuary at 6.40. We went up to Bontddu. I declined to go higher because in returning it would be rougher. The party landed at Bontddu. I spoke to William Jones... and advised that they should not go further than Bontddu. My party started back at 8.30. William Jones and his party in the "Jane" started back before me. I gave orders to the steersman in my boat to keep alongside the shore. When we got to Farchynys it was getting choppy and I told him to keep nearer the shore. William Jones's boat had rounded the point and was out of sight. He kept the boat quite close to the shore. My boat shipped a little water in rounding the point. I gave instructions to the

gentleman who steered to keep the boat slantways, and we were making for the shore. I did not see the "Jane." I made for the shore and landed the five passengers. ... I put my party out because of the danger. The party stayed longer at Bontddu than I wanted them to stay.

This is a revealing detail. The gold mine visit had taken longer than Lewis Edwards had anticipated, and to start the return journey as late as 8.30 was already risky as it would soon have been getting dark. However, to his credit Edwards recognised and responded to the danger by returning to the Bontddu jetty to land his passengers.

The one local passenger, a Miss Edwards of Barmouth,[11] is reported as saying she changed boats at Penmaenpwll, a reporter's error for Bontddu, as only one boat went as far as Penmaenpwll. She must have made the upriver journey in William Jones's boat as there is no suggestion that Paton and Gray's boat put in to Bontddu. She gives a vivid account of the aborted attempt to return in the "Rosa":

I went up the Mawddach in one of the other boats, but at Penmaenpool [Bontddu] I was persuaded to enter Edwards's boat. We had it pretty smooth until we got to the point called Ynyspridd, a little below Bontddu. The waves at this point ran high and wild, and I never experienced such tempestuous weather. Our boat was hurled to and fro, and we could not for some time make any headway at all. After considerable difficulty, however, we reached the shore safely. On two or three occasions our boats seemed completely under water, and our escape was marvellous.[12]

After putting five of his passengers ashore, Lewis Edwards set off to row back to Barmouth with the sixth who was lame. One of his passengers also gave evidence at the inquest:

William Henry Read, one of the party in Captain

Edwards's boat, said that it was very rough all the way up to Bontddu,[13] where they were landed, and after visiting the gold mine they started back. Finding the water so rough, they pulled ashore, and, with the exception of one, walked to Barmouth. In answer to Inspector Jones, Read said that none of the party visited the Halfway Inn.[14]

This was the group which arrived back first on foot to Barmouth. The exception was Charles Edward Harrison of Derby, 'the lame gentleman who was brought back by one of the boatmen,' and who gave evidence which 'bore out that of the boatman.'[15]

In the hours after the accident there had been an allegation from a woman visitor to Bontddu (the wife of a Liverpool cotton broker) that the accident was due to some of the party being drunk. She had been persistently spreading the rumour in Barmouth's shops. This caused a furore. 'Evidence was given amongst others by Mr. Prior, of Hastings, who was in the same boat as Mr. Newman, and who declared that all the party were perfectly sober, and that the upsetting of the boat was purely accidental.'[16] The woman concerned later presented a statement of apology to the Coroner's court via her husband, acknowledging that her hastily formed opinion had no foundation and regretting the distress caused. That one of the group was lame seems to have given rise to the error. William Jones acknowledged that he had been hungry and had bread and cheese at Bontddu's Halfway Inn, but nothing to drink. All the National Home Reading Union members, it was agreed, were teetotallers. Rev. T. A. Leonard asked the Coroner to ensure that the damaging rumour was officially quelled with as much energy as it had been disseminated. It is a reminder how vulnerable we have always been to 'fake news' and how assiduously we need to expose it.

William Jones tells what happened to the "Jane" on the return journey:

The wind was against us. Seeing that the sea was getting rough, and observing that some of the rowers were not very skilful I requested them to cease rowing. I then managed the boat very well. As we were turning round a sharp corner, however, one of the party sitting at the stern of the boat lost his hat and turned back to look after it. This caused the boat to roll slightly. The water rushed in, and the next instant the boat was swamped. I had already turned towards the shore, and we were within seven or eight yards of land.... In my opinion nothing whatever could have happened to our boat had the party at the stern not turned round when his hat was blown off.[17]

However, if such a simple move as a passenger turning to look back could upset the boat, it is clear that it was already at great risk of capsizing. The boat was only a few yards from the shore when the disaster happened as William Jones by his own account had turned towards the bank, presumably very aware of the danger. It is hard to avoid the conclusion that his testimony seems designed to present himself in as positive a light as possible.

Survivors of both boats speak of rounding a headland and meeting the full force of the wind, and 'boiling' or 'surging' waters. Each boat would have come from the relatively narrow and sheltered stretch of the river out into the broad expanse of the estuary by Farchynys, exposed to the full force of the south-westerly gale from the sea. Not only would they have come out from behind the twin headlands into a mile-wide stretch of water, but at this point the main course of the river crosses from the south to the north of its bed, just where the narrows open out. The rowers would have encountered not only a fierce headwind but disastrously turbulent water where the river at its narrowest point, moving from south to north, was roughed up by a wind at right angles to its flow. When the tide rises in conflict with the river flow, as it does twice a day, complex currents are always created, particularly at this spot. Add a south-westerly gale to the situation, and the so often peaceful river becomes a deathtrap. On the evening of 1 August 1894 the Mawddach by Farchynys must have been a maelstrom. In addition, since it was nearly dark, the chances of a good outcome were minuscule.

Frederick Pryor's evidence to the inquest was revealing. He was in William Jones's boat, the boatman wielding two oars in the bow and the other men – himself, his friend John Newman, Herbert Woodworth, and Mr Fildes (or Fields) – taking turns with one oar each and steering. Although 'the sea was choppy and the wind high' he said, 'We went upstream easily, wind and tide with us.... We enjoyed the row up to Bontddu.' After the visit to the gold mine the return journey was a different matter. There were, he said, five in the stern of the boat:

> The stern was low in the water. We started about 8.30 with the wind and tide against us. The sea was rougher, and it was hard work to row the boat. When the accident happened I was at the oar, and I noticed the boat roll a good deal, and that the waves were high. The first thing I remarked was that the water was rushing from the bow of the boat under my feet. Then more water came in until the boat got swamped. I jumped out and struck for the shore. I am not a swimmer but I have been taking lessons since I came to Barmouth. My watch stopped at 17 minutes to nine.

The light must have been fading fast.

William Jones continues:

> I was pitched into the water and swam ashore. When I got ashore I secured a boat and went out immediately to rescue the party. My boat was floating upside down. I found one person clinging to the keel of the boat, and I picked him up safely. I then found another clinging to a

piece of wood, and I rescued him. We then noticed two ladies floating, and the two men who were with me got hold of them and we went ashore. When we landed one lady was unconscious, and all our efforts to revive her failed.

Frederick Pryor tells how he held on to a plank and was rescued by Jones after about twenty minutes:

Mr Fildes and the boatman were in the boat. The latter pulled towards me and I got in. Mr Fildes then got hold of one of the Miss Reeds and I saw the body of the other Miss Reed floating, and I clutched hold of it, but she had her face downwards. I held it out of the water and we rowed ashore. We put Miss [Marie] Reed on the sands and tried to restore her. Miss Reed [Marie's sister Maud] tried first and then I tried all I could to restore animation. She, however, seemed to be dead.

Mr. Fields reported his own parallel experiences to the Press Association the day after the accident:

The ten drowned were staying in the house in which I am at present, Hendre Villas. We came down here on a trip which had been arranged by the Home Reading Union. We started up the Mawddach river yesterday evening and went as far as the gold mine. We had experienced boatmen with us, and the water was not at all rough. We started back at about a quarter past eight. There were several boats. I was in the first, the sea was smooth enough until we got to a point named the Little Island [Farchynys perhaps, which may have been mistaken for the Welsh for 'Little Island'], where there was a sharp curve. The boatman told us to put our oars down, and leave the steering and everything to him. In an instant a big wave rolled over us, swamping the boat, and casting us into the boiling waves. I could not swim, but I managed to turn on my back and float. I saw the boat upside down. The next thing I remember is being in the bottom of the boat, the boatman having pulled me in. I looked round and caught sight of Mr. Pryor, and got him to stick to the boat. Then I saw Miss Read [Reid], who had hold of a sister of her's. I got hold of one of the Misses Read, and held her up until I was almost exhausted. I then tried to get hold of her sister but failed, so I clung to one only. Mr. Pryor got hold of the other, and the boatman made for the shore, but I could not get the head of Miss Maud Read [Marie Reid] above water, and despite all efforts she perished. It was then almost dark. We saw a light in the distance and we made for it across the marshes, stone walls, and ditches, carrying the surviving Miss Read with us, and leaving the others on the shore. When we reached a farmhouse every hospitality was shown us. After Miss Read recovered consciousness, we went back and managed to reach home safely. I may mention that there were seven of us in the boat, and that of the passengers only myself, Mr. Pryor, and Miss Read are now alive. It was a dreadful experience.[18]

The abandoning of the body of Marie Reid on the shore in near darkness as those who had barely escaped with their lives carried her unconscious sister laboriously across the rough wet ground to the farmhouse for help is a terrible scene.

However, it seems that at least the grief-stricken young woman who nearly drowned like the younger sister she tried so desperately to revive was eventually driven back to Barmouth in some sort of vehicle, presumably belonging to the farm, with the other survivors from William Jones' boat, Mr Fields and Frederick Pryor.

Meanwhile Lewis Edwards who was rowing his lame passenger, Charles Edward Harrison, back to Barmouth, found himself confronted with the unexpected:

In going along I saw an oar in the water and the gentleman picked it up. I afterward found that it belonged to the "Jane." Having proceeded a little further I saw a boat upside down from 10 to 20 yards from the shore. It was dark and I could not see well. About 200 yards further down I saw Wm. Jones in a boat. He shouted out that his boat had sunk, and that some of the party had been drowned, and that he had one body on the beach.

William Jones told the inquest that the accident to the "Jane" had 'happened close to the Caerdeon coalhouse, known as Mr Jelf's[19] boathouse, and from eight to ten yards from the Bontddu shore.' When the boat was swamped he swam ashore: 'I found a boat on the beach, took it, and rowed to the scene of the accident where I found the "Jane" bottom upwards. The anchor was down. The tide was running down strong. The boat had capsized between the tide and the eddy.' Those precious minutes while he swam, and searched ashore for another boat, and rowed it back to where his had capsized – however sensible and valiant a course of action – tragically were too much for three of his passengers in the water. If he had realised the urgency of the danger and turned back as Lewis Edwards had done, all might have survived.

The tide had now turned and was on the ebb. Lewis Edwards having landed most of his passengers took William Jones into the "Rosa." They went to where Marie Reid's body lay and further efforts were made to revive her, without result.

Once more events took an unexpected turn. Lewis Edwards takes up the narration:

After about a quarter of an hour we heard screams in the water nearly opposite to us. We could not tell whether it was the scream of one or more – whether proceeding from a man or a woman. It was then dark. William Jones and I put out to the place where we thought the screams came from. We shouted, but received no reply and could not see anything. I think it would then be a quarter past nine. We returned to the place where we left the lame gentleman and others with the dead lady and put the body in Thomas Garnett's boat,[20] made it fast to my boat; and William Jones and I rowed down the river. After going about a mile we heard a scream between us and the shore. I then took the oars and William Jones went to the bow to look out when he saw a lady in the water right ahead of us. She was floating on one of the seats of the boat. We got her into the boat and brought her to Barmouth.

The testimony of William Jones also made clear by how slender a chance Ethel Packer had been saved at all. He and Lewis Edwards had returned to the body of Marie Reid which had been left on the shore:

We heard someone calling out in the water, and Lewis Edwards and I set out in his boat in the direction where we had heard the voice and failed to see anybody. It was getting rather dark then. It would be from 9.30 to 10.... We put the body from the shore in the boat and brought it to Barmouth in Lewis Edwards' boat. We heard shouts and saw a lady in the water. That would be about an hour after the accident to the "Jane." We got the lady into the boat and she told us that she had been to Penmaenpool in a boat. She spoke after being taken into the boat, but got feebler as we approached Barmouth. We landed her and she was taken to Evan Edwards's house[21] and attended to there. We picked up the lady about 500 yards nearer to Barmouth than where the accident happened to the "Jane."

The two boatmen began to realise that 'she belonged to Mr. Paton's boat, she evidently being the only survivor.'

The two boats of the experienced boatmen had lost sight of the third early on. It was only at this point that they realised what had happened to it – that the Oxford rowers' boat had gone right on to Penmaenpwll where they had had tea before setting out on the return journey which ended in disaster. Paton and Gray were perhaps expecting the other two boats to join them there, as Mathias Hubbard suggests the initial plan for everyone was to go to Penmaenpwll. The Barmouth boatmen had declined to go that far – it would have been a foolhardy trip to embark on so late in the evening even in good weather – and put in to Bontddu, a much shorter trip. William Jones said he started back at about 8.30: 'The "Margaret" was not then in sight. She passed us at Bontddu and that was the last I saw of her.' It must have been even later when the "Margaret" at Penmaenpwll set off on the return journey. Paton and Gray seem not have noticed how late it was getting or they could have cut short the tea party. As darkness fell, it removed the chance that someone on land might notice a boat capsize and come to the rescue.

As it turned out, the only person who had tea at Penmaenpool and survived, indirectly owed her life to the capsizing of William Jones' boat, as the sole reason he was returning downriver at that spot and at that late hour was that he had spent an hour rescuing people from his own boat and attempting to revive Marie Reid, before heading back to Barmouth in Lewis Edwards' boat with her body. It was as they were doing this that they heard her cries and found Ethel Packer clinging to one of the thwarts which made seats in the boats. She was being carried downriver on the now falling tide towards the sea.

The inquest was adjourned until the Friday afternoon. At that hearing Mr Harrison was giving evidence when the only survivor of William Paton and Percival Gray's boat arrived:

The Coroner, upon seeing Miss Packer entering the room, asked witness to kindly give place to that lady as he was anxious not to detain her under such trying circumstances.

It seems extraordinary nowadays that not much more than twenty-four hours after she was rescued, Ethel Packer was expected to present her evidence to the Coroner's court.

The story of the boat rowed by William Paton and Percival Gray has yet to be told. Ethel Mary Packer of Leeds, its sole survivor, was the only one who could give an account of what happened to the inquest, an account which was reported in graphic detail in the papers:

She stated that on Wednesday evening she was in one of the boats that went up the river, the same boat in which Messrs. Gray and Paton and Misses Moore, Malinson [Mallison], Golightly, and Greenwell were. They left Barmouth Harbour at about twenty minutes to seven, the river at that time not being very rough. She knew that both Mr. Paton and Mr. Gray were accustomed to boating. The passage to Penmaenpool was accomplished without any mishap of any kind, and they landed and had tea at the hotel there. Both tide and wind were in their favour going up. During the first part of the return journey the water was comparatively calm, but after they had proceeded three or four miles it suddenly became very rough. A big wave came into the boat, and witness asked Mr. Paton if there was anything to bail with. He replied, "Use my hat." Miss Malinson was just stooping down to do so, when another big wave dashed forward and swamped the boat, with the result that they all got into the water. At first they all went down together, but when witness came up the first time she clung to a piece of wood, which she believed was thrown by one of the gentlemen. The others were struggling in the water. She saw one of the gentlemen holding a lady up on his arm. Witness heard Miss Moore shout "Can you find the boat," and she also heard Mr. Gray cry for "help." They seemed to be a long distance from shore – in mid-stream, as near as she could guess. She floated by the aid of a plank, and remained in the water some time. She afterwards became unconscious, and did not remember being rescued and taken to Barmouth. It was never suggested when they started out from Barmouth that it was too rough for them to venture out. The only remark she heard was one about it being late when they would arrive back. Mr. Grey was stroke oar, Mr. Paton was also rowing, and Miss Moore was steering.[22]

The Derby paper also reported her evidence:

Miss Packer, the lady who was picked up a mile down stream, stated that she went up the river in a boat with Messrs. Gray and Paton and four others. They proceeded as far as Penmaenpool, passing other boats quickly. They started back with the tide against them. When three or four miles down the river the water became rough. One wave made four inches of water. They baled this out with Mr. Paton's hat, then a second wave came and swamped the boat. They had then got to a wide part of the river. All were turned into the water, and went down. Miss Moore had her arms in witness's. Coming to the surface a piece of wood caught her face. She thought the wood was pushed to her by one of the gentlemen, who were still struggling in the water. She saw one gentleman holding one of the ladies in his arms, and heard Miss Moore call out, "Can you find the boat?" Witness heard nothing more. Mr. Paton and Mr. Gray also called for help. She then drifted away from the others, and remained floating by means of the plank for a long time. She remembered nothing as to being taken out of the water. Mr. Paton gave orders to Miss Moore, who was steering, to turn the boat to land. Soon after the boat was swamped.[23]

The Leeds press reported her lucky escape in poignant detail:

One of the ill-fated party who went out boating on

Wednesday evening was Miss Ethel Packer, daughter of Mr. William Packer, Clerk to the Leeds School Board. She had been staying with her aunt (Miss Packer)[24] at Barmouth. The following is an extract from a letter which Mr. Packer has just received from this lady: – My very dear brother, – This is a terrible occurrence, but we may all feel devoutly thankful that our share in it was not greater. Ethel was the only one saved in the boat she was in. I am very much afraid the two gentlemen lost their lives in trying to save the ladies. They were both such fine fellows, and so thoroughly unselfish. Dr. Paton's son was more than six feet high, and a splendid rower and swimmer. He was found entangled in the ropes of the rudder. The other was a young fellow from Oxford, and looked about twenty years of age. He was just going to take his degree, and afterward become a clergyman in the London slums. There were three boats, two under the care of a boatman. Two girls from Durham, who slept in our room, and were in Ethel's boat, were found clasped in each other's arms. Their name was Golightly. I believe they were thoroughly Christian girls, both quite young, and individual Home Readers. Miss Moore, a young lady who was also in Ethel's boat, has not been recovered yet. Ethel thought so much of her. She thinks she clung to the same piece of the boat, and as the weight of both took it under, she believes Miss Moore voluntarily let go. She was quite equal to such a thing... They were all up the estuary, three miles from the bay, and the water was quite calm till they tried to get to the side and there it was more dangerous than the sea itself. Ethel was brought to a house on the quay and a doctor was fetched. She was quite unconscious for a good while, but she was coming round when I got there. She is excessively distressed.[25]

It is extraordinary that she was able to give the Coroner coherent evidence of what had happened so soon afterwards.

Her testimony is revealing. It seems William Paton, alarmed at the amount of water entering the boat in the turbulence as they passed through the 'gap,' told Edith Moore at the rudder to turn the boat to the shore. It proved a catastrophic decision. The boat went side on to wind, waves and current and was immediately swamped. Away from the shore in near darkness with a gale blowing, there was little hope their cries would be heard or that they would be seen and rescued. It remains remarkable that even one of the eight in the boat survived.

In fact the capsizing of both boats followed a similar manoeuvre. Turning broadside on for the shore was disastrous. William Jones' boat was already close to the shore and not far from that of Lewis Edwards, but even so three lives were lost. Once it had capsized the prompt action and skills of the two boatmen meant that as many were saved, but it remains questionable whether the excursion should have been embarked on in the first place, or that the return journey from Bontddu should have been attempted by experienced boatmen who knew the dangers well.

The fact that Lewis Edwards decided to turn back from the return journey so that all of his passengers who could walk returned safely to Barmouth on foot speaks volumes about how conditions deteriorated as the evening wore on.

At the inquest William Jones was singled out for praise for his conduct – which, once his boat had been swamped, was undoubtedly courageous and constructive – but it could be argued that of the two experienced local boatmen it is Lewis Edwards who was the most commendable. Again, reluctantly, it has to be borne in mind that the Coroner and his jury would have been aware of the impact the disaster could have on the area's reputation and prosperity, and as part of the structures of local officialdom they would have wished to avoid painful scrutiny from afar. They may have been as keen to deflect criticism from the boatmen as they were themselves.

Lewis Edwards even set out upriver once more in the

night with his two sons to help the recovery of the bodies. His was the third boat to set off on the search, while a policeman walked along the shore. The *Cambrian News* continued the story:

> The body of Mr Paton was found washed up onto a bank. The other seven bodies were found floating in the water. At that time the search party was not aware that two boats had been swamped, and thought it strange that the "Margaret" had not returned from Bontddu. Eventually, however, the party in searching for more bodies, found the "Margaret" upside down about 200 yards further up the estuary than the "Jane" which was also found upside down. The anchors of each boat had fallen out on the capsizing of the boats, and both were at anchor near the spot where they were swamped.

That afternoon another search party went upriver and dragged the sandy bottom for several hours but found nothing other than a hat and a pair of boots.

In the event it was not until the Saturday afternoon that the body of John Newman was found 'in the upper reaches of the river,' having been spotted from a train. It had presumably been carried further inland on subsequent rising tides.

That of Edith Moore was never recovered.

The Aftermath

The adjourned inquest resumed: 'Robert Morris, a boatman, gave evidence as to the recovery of seven bodies near the spot where the boats were capsized. Two boats were laying [sic] on the sand bottom upwards.'[26]

Captain Lewis Edwards, master mariner, stated that nothing was said to him when they started about how far they were going. In answer to the Coroner, witness said all the members of the party appeared to be tee-totallers.

The Rev. T.A. Leonard (General Hon. Secretary, National Home Reading Union)[27] asked the Coroner's permission to make a statement. He wished to acknowledge the bravery and courage of Captain William Jones, but for whom the sadness of the fatality would have been intensified. He expressed the deep appreciation of all the relatives of the deceased persons for the kind sympathy manifested on all sides. With regard to Messrs. Gray and Paton, who were both excellent swimmers and of splendid athletic proportions, he firmly believed that they had sacrificed their lives in attempting to save others. He wished to strongly repudiate any suggestion that any one of the party walked unsteadily, as it was absolutely untrue.[28]

The allegation that alcohol had played a part was clearly still circulating despite the evidence given. The young temperance-minded passengers were perhaps unlike other holidaymakers.

It was also Rev. Leonard who put some pointed questions to the inquest about the local authority's regulation of boating at Barmouth. Both boatmen had held licences the previous year but not the current one. Officials produced copies of bye-laws, but it turned out they had been printed but not circulated. These were local administrative weaknesses rather than serious matters, but they were indicative of a problem at the heart of local and national government responsibilities.

As the news broke across the country, with the extended inquest covered in detail in national and provincial papers from the north of Scotland to Cornwall, it quickly evoked a response. Many people remembered happy times in Barmouth and were touched by the tragedy.

There were also some serious questions to be answered.

As early as 7 August Rev. C.W. Carrington was raising some issues which must have been in many people's thoughts:

> During a recent stay at Barmouth it was a constant topic of wonder to myself and friends that so few serious accidents occurred to the crowds of competent and incompetent excursionists by water. The incompetent are liable to meet with accident anywhere, but the best of rowing men cannot navigate the Mawddach estuary safely in the boats that are generally on hire at Barmouth. These are mostly of a type adapted for an ordinary river, or for the Barmouth estuary in the fairest weather; but no one starting up the river for a long row can reckon on the state of the water in two hours' time. I have myself experienced a sudden change of wind, when sculling in a small boat, which rendered it impossible to cross the estuary for an hour or more without the certainty of being swamped. This was of no consequence to me personally, as I was not in a hurry, and should not have been the worse for a swim. But it is a very risky business to send out a large party in a boat well fitted for the Thames, but liable to be swamped by rough water, and the Barmouth estuary can change into a surging sea in ten minutes. The rush of water through the piers of the bridge at high tide, even when calm, is quite sufficient to overset a low-built boat if unskilfully managed. There can be no real safety for large parties of non-swimmers on the estuary unless real sea-going boats take the place of the light craft now entrusted to everybody.[29]

On 10 August the *Cambrian News* included a special supplement about the disaster, and a reflective piece:

> The marvel is, not that there has been an accident, with lamentable loss of life, but that there are not more of these accidents all up and down the coast. Even at Aberystwyth the tendency is to put slighter boats on the

beach every year. Fears are laughed at, and the people who risk their lives come back time after time to heap ridicule upon the cautioners.... Caution is silenced, and risks are run which only now and then end as the excursion up the Mawddach ended....

The only question worth asking now is whether the estuary of the Mawddach should be treated in future as if it were a lake, and whether visitors are to be sent out on the open sea in boats that may repeat the Barmouth disaster any day.[30]

On 18 August the *North Wales Chronicle* reported a letter from "A Welsh Boating Man" developing the point. He wrote that 'the class of boat mostly used at Barmouth is not at all suited for tidal waters' and that 'the boats which are wanted for the Mawddach and its estuary are not Oxford skiffs, but light sea-going boats like a yacht's gig.'

A photograph of half a dozen passengers in John Morris's boat gives an alarming indication of how low in the water such boats must have been, even in the calmest weather.

The inquest did hear technical evidence about the condition of the boats and the regulations in relation to their operation but found no culpability. It was accepted that the eighteen-foot boats were not overloaded and the boatmen were exonerated. William Jones in particular was commended for his actions in saving lives: 'The jury unanimously commend the behaviour of Capt. William Jones after the accident, and also the discretion shown by Capt. Lewis Edwards in landing his passengers and for his active assistance.'

Discretion – implying discerning good judgment – is a key word, a quality which was conspicuous for its absence most of that evening.

The inquest recommended that the licensing of boats should be tightened and the number to be carried clearly advertised, but it stopped short of requiring a boatman to be present.[31] It also recommended that 'an Inspector should be employed by the Local Board who should warn persons of the danger they incur in boating in the Estuary, in certain conditions of wind and tide, by the hoisting of a flag or in some other manner, as well as to enforce the Local Board's Bye-laws in regard to boating.'

A verdict of accidental death was returned: 'That the deceased were accidentally drowned by the swamping of boats whilst boating in the River Mawddach, in the parish of Llanaber, on the first day of August instant.' Later a similar verdict was returned by the inquest into the death of John Newman which was held at the County Hall in Dolgellau.

The lack of experience of William Paton and Percival Gray in any other than calm inland waters, however expert they were as oarsmen, clearly contributed to the tragedy, but the overall sequence of events, including the boatmen's roles, demonstrates that although it was an accident, it was one that might have been anticipated and avoided. Nonetheless it is surprising to see seven years later a cluster of the same boats at the prow of the supply ship *Dora* from Liverpool on one of her regular visits to Barmouth in 1901. Evidently little had changed.

Thankfully it is now many years since there were boats for hire to amateurs in Barmouth harbour.

Sadly other tragic events followed those of August 1894. Ethel Packer, the only survivor from the boat rowed by William Paton and Percival Gray, died just five years later aged 23.

Then in August 1898 Home Reading Union members up and down the land heard of a further disaster, chillingly familiar:

Derwentwater was the scene yesterday of the most distressing boating disaster. About sixty members of the National Home Reading Union are holidaying near Keswick; and on Friday morning a party of them started on an expedition to Watendlath. In crossing the lake one of the boats containing eight persons was capsized, and five ladies of the party were drowned before help could be rendered... The circumstances of yesterday's tragedy are particularly painful, and recall those of the disaster at Barmouth a few years ago, when a sad accident happened to a boating party also composed of members of the Home Reading Union at the mouth of the Mawddach.[32]

Lewis Edwards, an immensely experienced middle-aged boatman, the only one whose boat did not capsize on the fateful evening of 1 August 1894, was himself to die a few years later in a similar tragic accident. He took Clement Lowe, from Coesfaen, now known as the Clock House, which makes such a picturesque landmark in the estuary, out on a fishing trip on an August afternoon in 1900.

Charles Stuart (1838-1907), 'The Estuary, Barmouth.'[33]
Coes Faen does not yet have its clocktower.

It was something they had done together for twenty years, whenever Clement, whose father had a chemicals factory near Stockport, was staying at the family's holiday home. Both were equipped with waterproofs and boots as the weather was not good. When it became suddenly violently squally, Edwards decided they should make for shore, but the little sailing dinghy was unable to withstand the mounting waves and capsized. Lowe, in his thirties, managed, just, to swim ashore clutching an oar, but Edwards, an older man in his sixties, was drowned.

His impressive monument in Llanaber churchyard, a white marble column topped with a draped urn, makes no mention of how he died, or, unusually for Llanaber, of his maritime career – or of his other life as a greengrocer in the centre of Barmouth. The inscription reads simply: 'In loving memory of Lewis Edwards, the beloved husband of Miriam Edwards, St. Anne's Square, Barmouth, who departed this life August 6 1900 aged 62 years.' The grave is to the left of the main path to the church door, just before the first side path left. Its immediate neighbour, with an anchor in a roundel at the top of a grey stone, is the resting place of a fellow sailor, who died the very next day – Captain Evan Jones, of Min-afon, Barmouth, who was aged fifty-four, and whose name had featured in

The memorial to Lewis Edwards

the inquest to the 1894 disaster. Though the Harbour Trust had offered a vote of sympathy to him in his illness in mid-July,[34] it is hard not to wonder if the news about Lewis Edwards in some way precipitated his demise.

William Jones, who had captained the boat which had capsized after leaving Bontddu and had succeeded in rescuing some of his passengers though not all, lived on. At the 1911 census he was 75, a widower and 'Retired Master Mariner' living at Pen y Cei at the end of the quay with his sister-in-law Jane Jones, 59, her 16 year-old son named William, and another brother David, 55, who was down as a 'Ship Owner.' All were recorded as speaking Welsh rather than English. On 28 November 1916 William Jones of Penycei was buried at Llanaber at the age of 80, the burial 'Certified by Captain Jones,' perhaps a brother.[35]

It makes a fitting conclusion to this part of the sad story that a poet who knew and loved Barmouth was moved to write a poem about it. H. D. Rawnsley, a Canon of Carlisle, pioneer conservationist instrumental in founding the National Trust, friend of Ruskin and Beatrix Potter and a prolific sonneteer, may have been visiting his friend Fanny Talbot in Barmouth at the time. His sonnet's focus is the two young men who had organised the Reading Group holiday, but there were eight other young lives full of promise which were also cut short on that tragic day in 1894.

A River Tragedy

Barmouth

To the memory of the brave men Paton and Gray, who lost their lives in attempting to save others from drowning in the river Mawddach, 1st August 1894.

Old Caerdeon's brow is heather-bright;
From Dyfws far to Idris' purple chair
The heavens are cloudless blue, the noon is fair,
And every bay is filled with sapphire light.
Clouds fleck the heaven, and Cader fades from sight;
Dull grows the heather, sunless is the air;
The wind moans loud o'er shallows blank and bare,
And mournfully on Mawddach sinks the night.
Now Sorrow on from cape to headland wails;
And childless mothers weep along the shore
For those dear dead so silent on the sands;
But two bright stars have risen to set no more,
And Christ, the Saviour cries with wounded hands –
"Love, that will lose its life, alone avails."[36]

Perhaps H.D. Rawnsley's collections of sonnets were included among the books recommended to members of the National Home Reading Union. Hopefully the solace of poetry was of some comfort to the grieving families of 1894.

It was an era when early death was a depressingly familiar occurrence, but no more easy to accept than it is today when it is relatively rare. The Mawddach disaster clearly touched a national nerve. The particular poignancy of the loss of so many young lives, drawn from all over the country, symbolic of the best of futures, with their interest in books, ideas, and ideals, resonated in all

Hardwicke Drummond Rawnsley
(1851-1920)

communities. The innocence of a reading holiday in a beautiful part of the country, the simple attraction of a river excursion on a summer evening, underlined the fragility of all hope, and the ubiquity of grief. The fact that so many of these serious-minded, promising young people were not from privileged backgrounds but from ordinary, hard-working families, from ordinary, hard-working cities with harsh living conditions for so many of their citizens, struck an echo in many hearts. In this first era of rapid news delivery the tragedy was on everyone's lips. Everyone could relate to the idea of a holiday in a famously beautiful place like Barmouth, made accessible by train. Everyone also related to the idea of education as the ladder to self-improvement. And everyone related only too acutely to the fear of death, particularly the terrible loss of the young, the future. The special supplement published by the *Cambrian News* just ten days after the tragedy concluded with these still thought-provoking remarks:

Every year boating, mountain climbing, swimming, and other forms of pleasure-seeking claim their toll of human life, but it is only when the calamity comes home to us that its terrible nature is understood.

The bereaved are to be pitied with infinite pity. I have no doubt that as long as life lasts it will be saddened by the calamity that is probably only yet half realised.

There is nothing to say. Language has no words for these supreme experiences. Language is for everyday use in shops and markets, and at firesides and by the way. In crises we fall into silence. Grief and sorrow, total loss and sense of awe, are mocked by words.

Do we not all know of some things which if they happened to us would kill us. We might not die immediately, but the foundations of our life would be shaken. This event is of that nature....

To prevent repetition is all we can do, and perhaps not that. Life, perhaps, would not be worth living if we were not more or less reckless with it.

We cannot say wise words to the bereaved, but we can stand in sympathetic attitude and be silent while grief has its way.[37]

III

Retracing the Fateful Trip

The River Mawddach, Barmouth, Merionethshire

Arriving by Rail

Barmouth, of course, has no ancient castle though it might have seemed a suitable location for one.[1] The iconic place of medieval castles in the imagery – and imagining – of North Wales, such as Edward I's Harlech along the coast, or Welsh castles such as Cricieth across the bay and Bere on the south side of Cadair Idris, is supplied in Barmouth's case, it could

be argued, by the relatively recent railway bridge as icon. It is a different order of monument but one by which the town is likewise instantly recognisable. In 2004 it even featured on a stamp.

In 1894 all the National Home Reading Union visitors would presumably have arrived by rail across the bridge. Getting to Barmouth had long been difficult, particularly before the road from Llanelltyd was improved, but when the railway arrived it was 'all change' as travel from any part of the country could be achieved in a day.

The bridge – the longest surviving wooden viaduct in Wales today – was, shrewdly, built with a walkway alongside which remains available to pedestrians and cyclists. It has been called 'perhaps the finest artificial promenade in Great Britain.'[2] One of Barmouth's great tourist attractions is still the view up the 'sublime' estuary seen from the bridge footway, now toll free though for many years there was a small charge. A promenade across the bridge would no doubt have been a favourite of the Home Reading Union visitors too.

The clothes suggest this engraving[3] dates from the late 1860s shortly after the railway bridge opened, or possibly before, in anticipation of the new amenity, as the promenade appears wider than in reality (perhaps just artistic licence). The tall building on the left is Penrallt, initially one of the many hotels and guesthouses, still a Barmouth landmark in its prominent position between the road bend and the cliff, while visible in the distance is the distinctive outline of Coes Faen (its clock tower was added later), also perched between road and river.

Remarkably the view upriver has remained almost unchanged in the century and a half since the bridge brought the first train to Barmouth. Myths are also resistant to change. Idris, the giant whose seat was said to be the mountain Cadair Idris (Chair of Idris), was also a philosopher and astronomer whose profile is seen from this part of the estuary, his nose pointing to the sky in contemplation – he was 'Star-loving Idris' to the poet Robert Southey.[4] The boatmen would no doubt have pointed out the giant's profile to their Home Reading group passengers.

An Evening Excursion

Visitors have always been drawn to the sunsets over the sea, whether seen from the beach or mountain heights. In a mid-twentieth century postcard, from the hills on the opposite bank as the summer sun sinks over the sea, the isolation of Barmouth's island is stark.[5]

The railway viaduct connected Barmouth with the little station of Barmouth Junction, later renamed Morfa Mawddach, where the Cambrian Coast line via Machynlleth met the line from Dolgellau, now long closed, its curve clearly visible.

Evening on the estuary was – and is – deservedly famous for its atmosphere. The Liverpool artist Carleton Grant developed a distinctive style of watercolour, with pearly light – here suggesting moonlight – reflected on placid water, as in this 'art' card from the nineties.[6]

Perhaps postcards like this of evening light on the water may have been a spur to some of the young people to step into a rowing boat that evening of 1 August, despite the wind.

The hiring out of rowing and sailing boats gave a useful income to more and more people as the nineteenth century drew to a close, particularly mariners and fishermen who had spent decades going to sea, like Lewis Edwards and William Jones, who by their middle age had each accumulated enough money to buy a small boat or two and earn an independent living closer to home, a semi-retired life. The quay would have been crowded with boatmen as well as visitors when the National Home Reading Union group discussed their excursion plans. Eventually the decisions were made as to who would go, and in which boat.

Rowing boats in Barmouth harbour, 1898

They would have been in high spirits as they rowed out from the harbour. The original 'cock-and-draw' mechanism for opening the bridge was overhead when the three rowing boats negotiated the powerful currents between its piers, the first challenge on that fateful excursion, no doubt watched by bridge promenaders from above. It can be a high-risk affair in a small boat, even without a high wind.

Once clear of the bridge the three boats, probably now quite far apart, would have passed by Aberamffra harbour.

They would then have entered the wide stretch of water with the picturesque outline of Coes Faen at the tip of the left promontory. It is the first prominent landmark of the estuary looking upriver from the railway bridge.

Clock Tower
and Estuary, Barmouth

Barmouth Panorama.

Beyond it the river opens out in a mile-wide stretch, a favourite view from the Panorama Walk, reachable on foot from the centre of Barmouth, here appreciated by two women in white – before the narrows which lie ahead for boats going on to Bontddu or Penmaenpwll.

The Reading Union visitors would probably already have enjoyed an excursion to the Panorama Walk. The placid view could be deceptive. The wide expanse of water at high tide hides strong currents. It would have seemed so different from a small boat at water level.

At the inland end of the estuary the view west to the sea from the hills above Llanelltyd, a postcard favourite, gives an impression of the scale of the fateful excursion in 1894.

A sunset view of the estuary at low tide shows a maze of flows and eddies in the river's bed. The Coes Faen headland is the furthest one on the right. Bontddu village is behind the middle headland of the three.

The photograph reveals how at the narrowest point the main flow crosses from the southern headland to the northern one. This transverse flow was the crisis spot for the 1894 excursionists, in the face of a gale blowing straight up from the sea. Such wind conditions here, winter or summer,

often have gusts of up to 70 mph as we now know, but the science of weather measurement – and particularly forecasting – was then in its infancy.

At Bontddu the road which hugs the north bank for much of the estuary withdraws behind rocky hills, leaving the tidal shore wild and remote, haunted by water fowl, wind, and rustling reed beds.

The village of Bontddu which has always been part of Llanaber parish, Barmouth's parish, had acquired high status because of the mines above it. Clogau and Figra (pronounced Clog-eye and Vigra) were both producing gold in the 1890s, and a landing stage had been built to serve the industrial needs.[7]

As the weather deteriorated, two of the boats rowed from Barmouth on that first evening of August pulled in here to land their passengers, their boatmen knowing that to go on to Penmaenpwll so late in the day was unwise. The visitors then made the walk uphill to the gold mine on a beautiful track by a tumbling river.

Clogau mine, Bontddu, 1895[9]

One of the boatmen had a sandwich at the Halfway House[8] while his passengers were away.

The party would have looked around the Clogau mine with its substantial collection of buildings, all then in active production. They may even have met Robin, the bullion-carrying donkey.

Rhuddallt, Bontddu, 1947, view to the narrows with Barmouth bridge on the horizon

But by the time the two groups got back to their boats it must have been almost dark.

The third boat, the "Margaret," rowed by Paton and Gray, had pulled ahead of the other two early on, and was out of sight when the boatmen Lewis Edwards and William Jones decided to stop at Bontddu. With wind and tide still speeding their progress they passed the rocky promontory which screens Bontddu and continued upriver.

They would have passed Rhuddallt, a historic house on the shore east of Bontddu.

For the two rowers the view was back towards the sea, with the gap at the narrows narrowing further as the distance grew.

Although still tidal, the river now flows for a while between marshlands and reclaimed water meadows often grazed by cattle and sheep, before opening out again at the pool or harbour of Penmaenpwll, where ships had been built not so many years earlier.

In those days the railway line from Dolgellau to Barmouth ran right in front of the George III inn which was next to Penmaenpwll station. A wooden toll bridge was built

Penmaenpwll station

to replace a ferry in 1879, giving access to the station from the north bank and providing a still useful shortcut.

Now only the signal remains, kept as a reminder of the steam engines which chugged and whistled right next to the crowds of visitors from 1868 to 1965. The station building has been incorporated in the hotel, while the engine shed which used to be a few yards west has been demolished and the sidings turned into a car park. The signal box on the other

The George III inn by the toll bridge at Penmaenpwll

side of the toll bridge was also kept, and long served the RSPB as a look-out post to watch the water birds.

Paton and Gray pulled in here to land their boatload of young women before taking a well-earned tea at the hotel. Visitors to the George continue to sit outside and soak up the view.

One of those visitors was the poet Gerard Manley Hopkins (1844-1889) whose poem 'Penmaen Pool' is said to have been written for the visitors' book at the inn.

> from **Penmaen Pool**
> *Barmouth, Merionethshire, August 1876* [10]
>
> Who long for rest, who look for pleasure
> Away from counter, court, or school
> O where live well your lease of leisure
> But here at, here at Penmaen Pool?
>
> You'll dare the Alp? you'll dart the skiff? –
> Each sport has here its tackle and tool:
> Come, plant the staff by Cadair cliff;
> Come, swing the sculls on Penmaen Pool.
>
> What's yonder? Grizzled Dyphwys dim:
> The triple-hummocked Giant's Stool,
> Hoar messmate, hobs and nobs with him
> To halve the bowl of Penmaen Pool....
>
> The Mawddach, how she trips! though throttled
> If floodtide teeming thrills her full,
> And mazy sands all water-wattled
> Waylay her at ebb, past Penmaen Pool.
>
> But what's to see in stormy weather,
> When grey showers gather and gusts are cool? –
> Why, raindrop-roundels looped together
> That lace the face of Penmaen Pool....

And ever, if bound here hardest home,
You've parlour-pastime left and (who'll
Not honour it?) ale like goldy foam
That frocks an oar in Penmaen Pool.

Then come who pine for peace or pleasure
Away from counter, court, or school,
Spend here your measure of time and treasure
And taste the treats of Penmaen Pool.

Gerard Hopkins, reflected in a lake.
Aug. 14.

For all his seriousness, Hopkins could be light-hearted too, as this poem and his self-portrait sketch show.

Rowers and canoeists can still be seen on the river and a paddle sports festival is organised each September from Barmouth, but such activities are now carefully supervised and rowing boats are nowhere routinely for hire.

The former railway is now a popular footpath and cycle track known as the Mawddach Trail. Its course makes an ideal route from which to engage with the fateful 1894 excursion as along much of its length it hugs the river bank.

Catastrophe

It was at the narrowest point between the headlands west of Bontddu that all three boats separately met catastrophic conditions. The ebb tide was running down powerfully, but here the main flow runs not westwards but from south to north across the gap. The gale blowing at right angles to this current with fiercely squally gusts would have forced up the waters of the wider pool, flowing down through the narrows, into chaotic choppy waves. Both the professional boatmen knew that to hug the shore was the best option, but only one realised how dangerous the situation was and turned back

before his boat was swamped. The other had already capsized and the tragic consequences for three of his passengers were unfolding.

The inlet below Caerdeon was the scene of desperate efforts to revive Marie Reid, and then to get help for her now unconscious sister Maud, who was laboriously carried by people soaked to the skin, and themselves nearly drowned, across marshland and over walls.

Vegetation now covers the whole inlet west of the narrows, interwoven with tidal creeks. More of it would have been water then, but it would still have been a struggle for the men to carry Maud to the light of the unnamed farm, leaving Marie lifeless at the water's edge.

Further up the river at Penmaenpwll, on that fateful evening of 1 August 1894, by the time the party at the George were ready to get back in the boat for the two organisers to row them back to Barmouth, the tide had turned. They would have expected the ebb flow to help their return to the river mouth, but the wind had also strengthened and was set hard against them. Gale-force gusts were whipping up waves above the strongly running ebb tide with its turbulent currents. It was a dangerous cocktail of conditions, and it must already have been almost dark.

The old giant astronomer Idris watched the heavens impassively as the catastrophe struck:

> Idris, that, like warrior old,
> His batter'd and fantastic helmet rears,
> Scattering the elements wrath, frowns o'er his way,
> A broad irregular duskiness.[11]

As the morning light returned, the search parties who had been out all night eventually found the two upturned boats beached on the sand-banks which emerge at low tide.

The "Margaret" was a little way upstream. Ironically both were at anchor, as the anchors had fallen out as each capsized and had found a firm hold. Loose timbers such as oars and thwarts had also fallen out and thankfully saved some with their buoyancy. The group's leaders in the "Margaret," William Paton and Percival Gray, both swimmers it was reported, had no doubt done what they could, but there was little chance in those conditions of tide and weather as darkness fell that they could have saved either their passengers or themselves, even if they had been only yards from the shore.

William Jones in fact testified at the inquest that his boat was only eight to ten yards from the shore when it capsized, yet still three of his passengers died. The women's long skirts in particular must have been a fatal encumbrance, but from the way the body of one of the young men was found tangled in the mooring ropes of the "Margaret" it is evident that trousers were not necessarily a saving device either.

Ten families woke to terrible news on the morning of 2 August as telegrams were delivered. Parents and siblings rushed by rail from all over the country to grieve over the lost. As in the cover image here, they would have stood on Barmouth quay in the calm after the storm wishing they could make it all un-happen.

IV

Reflections on Risk and Safety

Barmouth's memorial cairn on the Somme centenary, 1 July 2016

Since the bronze age the skyline of Meirionnydd's mountainous landscape has been used to remember the dead. Countless cairns and other stone memorials skilfully placed on ridges and summits to be visible from far and near kept the memory of people alive to their successors.

Barmouth has its own more recent memorial cairn on Craig y Gigfran (Raven's Rock, also known locally as the Peak or the Flag) which commemorates the men of Birmingham who fell on the first day of the offensive which was to become known as the Battle of the Somme, 1 July 1916. In grief and without a grave to visit, some of their families got back on the train to visit the place of so many happy memories together, and climbing up to the skyline summit above the town, a favourite walk for so many, began to build a cairn.

Others added their own memorial stones so the cairn grew. The painted inscription at its base reads 'SOLDIERS FROM B'HAM DISTRICT WHO FELL 1 JULY 1916.'

Later a plaque with a similar inscription was fastened to a large rock at the summit. Today a Welsh flag streams from the cairn, clearly visible from the town and easily reachable from the centre after a steep climb.

At the centenary of that First World War battle in 2016, the Birmingham press carried a report on it and a few weeks later the city's lord mayor came to lay flowers on behalf of the people of Birmingham, an emotional moment.

Carl Rice, Lord Mayor of Birmingham, and Deputy Leader Ian Ward, August 2016

Though so different a ritual from that of a century earlier made by people who had lost those near and dear to them, the fundamentally positive nature of such a gesture is evident on the faces once it was completed. The rites of remembrance so often lead to relief.

Today we are even more aware of the need to remember, to commemorate, in our personal lives, but also as a community. In recent years the public centenary events for the First World War have shown an imaginative and beautiful response to the enormously painful subject, from portraits of the war poets marked out on tidal sands, to red ceramic poppies, one for each of the fallen, planted to fill the moat of the Tower of London. Key landscapes still hold real power to inspire and to heal.

At times we all need places to visit where we can reflect and remember, and from which we return in a better spirit, whether graves, places where ashes were scattered, or sites of other remembrance. It gladdens our spirits when others who did not know the person or people concerned are prompted to think of them.

But there is also a crucial place for official responses – whether coroner's report, formal inquiry, the definition of safety regulations, or the still ongoing address by historians to complex events such as World War I.

The memorial plaque in Llanaber Church to the ten who drowned that evening of 1 August 1894 speaks of the estuary as 'dangerous.' The wording was controversial with the local community,[1] no doubt fearful that the positive reputation of their town as an ideal holiday resort would be damaged, although the extensive and immediate coverage of the tragedy in newspapers throughout the country must have been in fact a far greater risk to Barmouth's image. The controversy is a reminder that vested interests may often play a part in how tragic events are reported, investigated, and ultimately remembered, and that we need to be vigilant about the risk of manipulation and distortion – by those being, in the famous phrase, 'economical with the truth.'

An extensive tidal estuary such as the Mawddach's must always pose dangers to do with the rise and fall of the tide against the flow of the river. The amount of water it receives from its catchment differs widely also between wet weather and dry – or icy, as some of the lowest river levels are seen in periods of prolonged frost. Today the river's main current changes from one side of the estuary to the other four times between Barmouth bridge and Penmaenpwll. Each of those cross currents will produce dangerous conditions at the surface, particularly in certain weather conditions such as a westerly wind, as on that fateful night. The boatmen and officials of Barmouth must have known they could not really deny that the estuary was dangerous.

Sadly accidents will always happen from time to time, but systems can be introduced to mitigate their harm. The founding of the national lifeboat charity in 1824 was a huge step towards limiting the loss of life on water. Barmouth responded from the beginning, establishing its first lifeboat in 1828. The name giving the familiar initials of the RNLI dates from 1854. Between then and 1865 its volunteer crews had saved sixty-one lives, a remarkable achievement. The first boat was replaced by the *Ellen* in the late 1860s and by the *Jones Gibb* in the late 1870s.

Rosalie Jones in her Barmouth history itemises some of the 'shouts' the *Jones Gibb* responded to, including a summer storm like that which led to the disaster of 1 August 1894:

The Jones Gibb *lifeboat, 1905*

In 1888 a yacht – the "Petrel" of Barmouth – was overtaken by a terrific storm on the twenty-seventh of July. Coming to the rescue with its usual indomitable pluck, the life-boat succeeded in saving the vessel and two lives. On the twenty-seventh of January 1890, a steamer from Glasgow named the "Maria" was in dire distress, but the Barmouth life-boat was able to render it valuable assistance by putting on board a pilot to guide the vessel safely out of the tempestuous bay. In April 1893 it rendered assistance in saving a ketch from Plymouth named the "Canterbury Bell;" and in March 1895 it brought ashore nineteen persons from the wreck of the four-masted barque from Liverpool named the "Andrada."[2]

Obviously much of the lifeboat's work was to assist larger vessels at sea. Unfortunately the three small boats which embarked in 1894 on an August rowing trip up the Mawddach as the evening light failed and the weather deteriorated had little chance of assistance from the lifeboat. There were no phones or pagers, and small boats would not have carried flares.

A further disaster at Penmaenpwll seventy years later was also beyond lifeboat help. A pleasure steamer bearing forty-two holidaymakers from Barmouth up the estuary on 22 July

1966 hit the toll bridge as it turned to berth at the George III Hotel.

Holed below the water line, it sank in very few minutes. The proprietor of the George had luckily taken delivery of a new small boat just five days earlier and acted with great presence of mind, with others, to rescue as many as possible from the water, but even so fifteen people were drowned.[3] The inquiry found that

> the loss of the *Prince of Wales* and the consequent loss of fifteen lives of her passengers was caused by the negligent handling of that boat by Edward Llewellyn Jones and because the *Prince of Wales* was inadequately manned.[4]

Jones was ordered to pay £100 towards the cost of the inquiry but was not found criminally liable. His brothers who were in partnership with him were also fined. Paragraph 9 of the report is revealing:

> Edward Llewellyn Jones is 73 years of age and has known the river Mawddach between Barmouth and Penmaenpool for over fifty years. He has had a lifetime of experience in handling boats, including many years as coxswain of the Barmouth lifeboat. Unfortunately his great experience led him to believe that he could navigate the *Prince of Wales* single handed. This belief was apparently shared by his brothers John Jones and Harry Lloyd Jones.

The vessel's licence, however, stipulated that it should be manned by two crew, and should carry no more than twenty-eight passengers, so it was both undermanned and overloaded. There were also doubts about whether the provision of life rafts met the licensed requirement.

The overriding key factor, though, which the 1966 official report identified was the dangerous overconfidence which can arise from experience. It chimes with the identical factor in the 1894 tragedy, overconfidence on the part of the group leaders, William Paton and Percival Gray, and the two captains, William Jones and Lewis Edwards. It is hard to escape the conclusion that the root causes of both disasters were sadly similar – which raises the question of whether the same risk may arise in future. Perhaps we should learn to build in wariness where experience and expertise are manifest, and to teach ourselves as individuals that where we are most confident we may be most at risk of catastrophic errors of judgment.

Nonetheless in extremis we all necessarily rely on the help of skilled and courageous people.

A story from 1908 illustrates both the skill and the bravery of a Barmouth man:

> A gentleman from Ruabon went bathing in front of Minymor on Friday morning, and after swimming seawards for some distance called for assistance. A heavy gale was blowing at the time and the tide ebbing, but Mr Hugh Davies, an attendant at the bathing machines, hearing the cry of the distressed bather, pluckily swam out and reached him in the nick of time. After a while both Davies and the bather managed to reach the shore in an exhausted condition. It was some time before the rescued gentleman could leave the shore for his lodgings. The bather had been cautioned not to go out so far. – Davies already holds the Royal Humane Society's medal.[5]

He must be the Hugh E. Davies who in 1901, at the age of just sixteen, was down as a general labourer and head of his household near the harbour, shared with his two elder sisters, their parents presumably having died. He clearly understood responsibility. Such valiant and selfless behaviour as seen in the saving of the man from Ruabon seems to have long been a quality of Barmouth folk.

The careers of local mariners were also keenly followed. In 1910 the local paper reported:

Barmouth. Maritime – Mr Harold Lowe has qualified as master mariner, and Mr Robert Lloyd Lewis youngest son of the late Captain Lewis, S.S. "Dora," as mate.[6]

Harold Lowe (1882-1944) was a son of George E. Lowe, described in one census as a 'Landscape and Cattle Painter,' who had run the Castle Hotel in Harlech with his wife Emma before moving to Penrallt, the prominent tall house on the headland where the road from the estuary enters Barmouth. His painting of Barmouth's supply ship *Dora* wallowing in a storm, on display in the Sailors' Institute on the quay, is a reminder of the force of the wind and the danger it brings.

George Lowe, 'SS Dora,' The Sailors' Institute, Barmouth

The cover artwork for this book also gives evocative expression to the idea of storm at sea – and shipwreck. It is by one of the established artists drawn to Barmouth in the 1870s, John Adam Houston (1812-1884).

Born at Gwydir, Llanrwst, he spent his early childhood in Wales before his family returned to Scotland. A member of the Royal Scottish Academy, he exhibited from 1841 to 1885 in Edinburgh and London, and although he moved to London in the late 1850s he continued to visit and work in both Wales and Scotland. By the early 1870s he was in his late fifties and at the peak of his career.[7]

Inscribed 'Painted for Mr Kinnear – Victoria – 1872' it was evidently commissioned by Robert S. Kinnear, an Australian, the son of a wealthy art collector in Melbourne, Victoria.[8] Whether the painting's subject was at Kinnear's behest or the choice of the artist can only be guessed. Either way, Houston's work – probably his sketch for the finished work in oil which may or may not survive – holds a remarkable tragic power.

Whether a particular incident is illustrated, or a general concept, is unknown. However, the local press in May 1871 carried this news:

> FOUNDERED AT SEA. – The schooner Ann, of Barmouth, Robert Roberts, master, on her passage from London to this port... when off New Quay Head encountered heavy weather, wind blowing fresh from the E.S.E.; the ship sprung a leak. The crew were then set to work at the pumps in hopes of keeping her afloat, but after getting within about two miles of Barmouth Bar it was found impossible to prevent her going down, and the captain ordered a boat to be got ready, and, after seeing the crew all safe in the boat, remained with the ship till the last minute. They had only time to get the boat from alongside the vessel, when she went down bow foremost. The captain and crew all landed safe at Barmouth.[9]

This could well have been the event which inspired J. A. Houston's drawing. The scene is clearly set on Barmouth's waterfront, with the quay and the Penrallt headland visible behind the young mother gazing out across the harbour bar, and there seems to be a mast in the distance which could well be that of the *Ann* in distress. Local people would have recognised the schooner, knowing it to be a local vessel, and helpless to reach their family members before it sank. Thankfully no lives were lost when that ship went down, but the fear in Houston's picture is palpable.

George Lowe's son Harold who qualified as a master

Painted for Mr. Hmum. Victoria – 1872

John Adam Houston, Drawing

mariner in 1910 went on to become famous as Fifth Officer of the ill-fated *Titanic*, who behaved with great professionalism and courage by commanding the only lifeboat which went back to rescue survivors. He was given a hero's welcome on his return to Barmouth and was presented with a gold watch by the people of Barmouth 'in recognition and appreciation of his gallant services.'[10] On the centenary in 2012 a plaque to honour his memory was unveiled on the wall of the Harbour Master's office at the end of the quay.

Yet his family's history is a reminder of the risks water poses. The Lowe memorial stone in Llanaber churchyard, perhaps erected by Harold, records not only the deaths of his parents – his father, 'Artist,'

Harold Lowe, Fifth Officer of the Titanic

lived at Penrallt until his death at 81 in 1928 – but also of two of his brothers. George, the eldest, named after their father, drowned at Barmouth on 27 December 1895 aged just seventeen. The inquest heard that after going across in his boat to Penrhyn he had returned, and after mooring his boat in Aberamffra harbour had gone home for his tea. Afterwards he went out again. When he did not return, a search was begun. His body was later found floating in the river near his boat. It was assumed he had gone back to check or move the boat, which was moored some way out, and had slipped in getting down from the quay and got into difficulties, although he could swim. The doctor reported no signs of injury. A verdict of accidental drowning was returned. His brother Edward was lost at sea in the equatorial mid-Pacific 'off the SS "Waitemata" on March 11th 1927 aged 33 years.' Harold, who survived the *Titanic* disaster, lived on to the age of 61 in 1944. He would have been just thirteen when George drowned in wintry waters at Barmouth, a family tragedy which perhaps led to his courage in rescuing *Titanic* survivors from the icy North Atlantic. As a lad growing up overlooking the estuary and no doubt used to messing about in boats with his brothers, he would also of course have been deeply affected by the loss of ten hopeful young lives on the Mawddach on 1 August 1894.

The family's gravestone is one of several at Llanaber commemorating mariners who died at sea, recording the latitude and longitude of the loss as if to fix the unfixable. Another is that for Richard, the son of Captain Griffith Evans and his wife Sarah, of 2 Aelfor Terrace, Barmouth, who died 'in Lat. 39 South Long. 170 West on July 16th 1904, aged 29 years, and was interred at sea on the 17th.' The location is in the South Pacific just east of the international date line and on the same latitude as New Zealand, a country served by SS *Waitemata*'s voyages. It is about as far from Barmouth as it is possible to be on this planet. Clearly the sons of Barmouth who went to sea saw the whole world, even if some did not return.

The slate headstone for Richard Evans stands against another, inscribed partly in Welsh, which records that the captain and his wife had already lost three of their children in childhood: an earlier Richard who died aged 3 in 1872, Owen Edward who died aged 6 months in 1875, and Salome who died aged 4 in 1888. The captain was one who knew the meaning of maritime coordinates and what it meant to travel the southern hemisphere near the Roaring Forties. The grieving couple had Richard's memorial carved with the following verse:

We cannot bend beside his grave
    He sleeps in the secret sea
And not one gentle whispering wave
    Will tell the place to me
But though unseen by human eyes
    Though mortals know it not
His Father knoweth where he lies
    And angels guard the spot.

In the context of this story, these simple words may perhaps be invoked as a memorial also to Edith Packer, one of the ten who drowned at Barmouth on 1 August 1894, the only victim of that tragedy whose body was never recovered.

It is abundantly clear that Barmouth's origins as a maritime community were still powerfully in evidence at the end of the nineteenth century and the start of the twentieth, and the commitment to and pride in her maritime traditions and heroes continue today.

In 2019 it was 125 years since the disastrous loss of life on the Mawddach in 1894, and in 2016 the fiftieth anniversary of the later Penmaenpwll tragedy was commemorated, but though these dire events could not be prevented, it remains a fact that throughout the more than two and a half centuries of the Barmouth lifeboat service, brave and selfless people have continued to save lives and to avert disasters whenever they could. The crews are still volunteers who put themselves forward into danger at all hours of day and night, and in all weathers, for the sake of others, a noble cause, rightly respected.

Today's lifeboat is a huge contrast to the early vessels such as the *Jones Gibb* with its dozen oarsmen. However, crewing them is often a family tradition that goes back many generations. The lifeboat station is now a substantial modern structure above the beach, designed to shelter the high-tech, high-powered vessel on its launch frame, towed by a tracked vehicle to draw it across the sand and into the water. In 2019 Barmouth RNLI took delivery of an impressive new lifeboat, the *Ella Larsen*, a £2.2m Shannon class vessel.

There is also a small inshore lifeboat. All those using the water in and around Barmouth can feel confident that they are protected as much as is humanly possible by the highly trained and valiant volunteers on call day and night to man these craft.

The new Ella Larsen *is tucked away by its launch vehicle, December 2019*

The air ambulance lifts off from Barmouth's football field with a patient
for Ysbyty Gwynedd, Bangor

SONNET

On the Dedication and Launching of the Barmouth Lifeboat
Lawrence Adern, *Stockport. August 8th 1939.*

To the deep waters of a restless sea
Do we commend this sturdy craft and true,
To serve our shores; and we could pray to Thee,
Lord of the raging tides, to give her crew
Storm-daring hearts, where ruthless Neptune vaunts
His might uncurbed; where gallant heroes sleep
Prostrate below, yet dream not in the haunts
Of tombless cemeteries in the dread deep.
Speed then, and combat death, pride of each hand
That hewed thy timbers into keel and prow
To cleave the tides and bring to haven-land
Storm-beaten souls. And as thy screws churn now
We know thou wilt most nobly serve our realm
When the great Master Pilot takes thy helm.

James Arnold Jones

The story of 1 August 1894 on the Mawddach also demonstrates the professional medical assistance of local doctors when the casualties began to arrive back at Barmouth. They tried so hard to revive those young lives. Nowadays as well as expert local doctors on hand and an ambulance service by road to the Accident & Emergency department at Bangor hospital,[11] there is also an air ambulance service which replaces the road journey of forty-eight miles with a flight of just a few minutes. The helicopter is frequently involved in airlifting injured climbers directly from the mountain slopes of Meirionnydd.

But sadly accidents can never be altogether prevented, particularly wherever there is water. In 2016 two young boys from Birmingham, aged fourteen and fifteen, were drowned while swimming off Barmouth beach, disappearing beneath the waves despite the efforts of beach wardens and friends, and before the lifeboat could reach them. The coroner, returning a verdict of accidental death, said they had experience of swimming pools 'but no experience of swimming in surf from an open beach.' He added, 'Just as there's no such thing as a safe mountain, there's also no such thing as a safe beach.' There's always a risk, he said, on beaches, and Barmouth was no less or greater than elsewhere

The Lord Mayor of Birmingham, Carl Rice, came to pay his respects,[12] handing over a wreath from the people of his city to the Mayor of Barmouth, Valerie McArdell, and the Lifeboat Operations Manager, David Baily.

As all parents know, there is a fine line between keeping children and young people safe and encouraging them to have an active and confident approach to life's opportunities. In the twenty-first century we live in an age when the enthusiasm for thrills despite risk is in direct conflict with the 'health and safety' culture. The Snowdonia National Park famously markets itself to visitors as the provider of

Carl Rice, Lord Mayor of Birmingham, hands his city's wreath for deposit on the waves in memory of the boys to the Mayor of Barmouth, Valerie McArdell, and David Baily, Lifeboat Operations Manager, 21 August 2016.

adventure holidays delivering uniquely exciting activities. Special facilities such as zip-wire runs and a surfing pool are directly under the control of authorities required to ensure safety for users, but the outdoor activities available everywhere informally, on water and land, cannot exclude risk.

Most people who cherish the beauty of wildness, on sea and land, would hate to see it withdrawn to a 'safe' distance. As adults, we want to make our own decisions, live our lives as we choose, building on our own experience, not as others dictate, even if nominally for our own good. The delight in nature in all her moods is precious to many. Too many warning signs may obtrude in beauty spots, and safety fences in certain circumstances can foster challenges as readily as compliance. And it is always true that anyone can fall anywhere in their own length and sustain serious injury, even at home – there is no need for a wild environment for it to happen. Nonetheless we all hope to return safely from holidays in some of the most beautiful and memorable places in the country, and the tragic, avoidable loss of ten young lives to the Mawddach on 1 August 1894 gives us all pause for thought.

Rosalie Jones wrote in 1907 of what drew great numbers of visitors to her area:

> At the present day the harbour and the beautiful Mawddach Estuary are used principally for the pursuit of pleasure in yachts or in small sailing or rowing boats. The magnificent scenery of the Estuary is not to be surpassed; and as the oarsman skilfully plies his oar, the spectator is wrapped in deep and silent admiration. Around him on every side rise vast mountains, or barren crags that overhang the water's banks, while the grassy slopes that rise from the river's edge are dotted here and there with picturesque abodes, and varied with spots of luxuriant verdure. In calm weather the glassy surface of the river is like a lake, and at such a time a sail at eventide

amid such scenery serves to picture to us more forcibly than any spirit of the imagination how the poets – Byron and Shelley – spent their hours of eventide upon Lake Leman, wrapt in contemplation of the glories of this world, and of the doubts and fears of the unknown world to come.[13]

The young author made no mention of the tragedy of 1894 when an evening river excursion in weather anything but calm ended in catastrophe, but perhaps her citing of this world's glories in the context of the uncertainties of the next would have evoked a poignant memory in many of her early readers.

Lifeboat crews will never be able to save all lives from the water any more than firefighters can prevent all loss of life from fire. But they make a huge difference by their selfless efforts. In the end perhaps the best we can do is remember quietly those who were lost, particularly the young full of promise, and those who wept for them, and honour the noble contribution of those who tried, and continue to try, to prevent such tragedies happening again.

On the edge of the harbour below the railway viaduct as trains emerge from the short tunnel through the rock to come in to Barmouth station is a stone sculpture. It was carved for the millennium by a local sculptor, Frank Cocksey, from a block of Italian marble raised from an early eighteenth-century wreck off the Meirionnydd coast. The story of the 'Bronze Bell'[14] wreck is now told in a museum on the quay housed in Barmouth's oldest building, Tŷ Gwyn.[15] It is thought the future king Henry VII met there with the local aristocrats from Cors y Gedol before making his bid for the throne of Richard III and founding the Tudor dynasty,[16] which gave the royal coat of arms the Welsh dragon opposite the lion before it was replaced with the unicorn of Scotland.

High-flown history apart, it is the small realities of maritime life which have shaped the character of the small

community by the Mawddach. Many lives must have been lost over the centuries, crossing the estuary's powerful currents in small boats. The sculpture, 'The Last Haul' or 'Y Llwyth Olaf,' gives moving representation to the drowned, but while it commemorates generations of fishermen, its central figure may also be seen as the hands of a mariner reaching to save.

Barmouth's quay is seen here from the marble sculpture under the railway viaduct on an August evening in 2016. The building above the slipway is where the casualties were brought on the night of 1 August 1894.

Frank Cocksey, 'Y Llwyth Olaf' or 'The Last Haul,' Carrara marble, 2000

John Masefield (1878-1967), who went on to be Poet Laureate from 1930, had been a sea cadet on HMS Conway, a training ship on the Menai Strait, and knew the weathers and dangers of Welsh waterways well, as this poem shows.

Cardigan Bay

Clean, green, windy billows notching out the sky,
Grey clouds tattered into rags, sea-winds blowing high,
And the ships under topsails, beating, thrashing by,
    And the mewing of the herring gulls.

Dancing, flashing green seas shaking white locks,
Boiling in blind eddies over hidden rocks,
And the wind in the rigging, the creaking of the blocks,
    And the straining of the timber hulls.

Delicate, cool sea-weeds, green and amber-brown,
In beds where shaken sunlight slowly filters down
On many a drowned seventy-four, many a sunken town,
    And the whitening of the dead men's skulls.[17]

The poem provides a poignant counterpoint to the tragedy of 1894. But the safe delights of a holiday in Barmouth and on the Mawddach are real and thankfully continue to be available.

The view from near the Clock House is still presided over by the profile of Idris the Giant, astronomer, philosopher and poet, while on Cardigan Bay, Barmouth's thirteenth-century church at Llanaber still keeps watch over the waters below.

The last word belongs to H. D. Rawnsley, who knits together the intense pleasure offered by a coastal walk on a beautiful summer's day, from Barmouth's estuary crowned by Cader Idris along to Llanaber, with a resonant reflection, prompted by a funeral taking place in the churchyard above, on the inevitable end which only strengthens the will to live:

> The sea was moveless azure in the bay,
> Yet the blue sea of Heaven was white with foam,
> As if the winds for mischief's sake would roam
> To steal the sense of too great calm away.
> Great Turra stretched a marvellous inlay
> Of wall and wood towards the Giant's home;
> And Hebog's hill, Carnarvon's bride, had come
> Across the waters in her veil of grey.
> I left the rushy hillocks, and I strolled
> Along the purple shore that pulsed with heat,
> To where Llanaber's fathers o'er the tide
> Sleep till the tides are not – a death-bell tolled –
> Rest for the weary-hearted ones is sweet,
> Dear God! to-day 'twere bitter to have died![18]

Notes

Chapter I

1. Pronounced 'M-ow (as in 'now')-th (as in 'this')-a-ch (as in Scottish 'loch'), the river did not always carry this name over its whole course. Early records refer to the tidal reach to Llanelltyd as the 'Maw' as perpetuated in the town's Welsh name, Abermaw, or the mouth (aber) of the Maw. Its two main tributaries are the Mawddach to the north and the Wnion to the north-east which come together at Llanelltyd, near the ruins of Cymer Abbey (Cymer means 'confluence'). The Wnion (which means 'straight') follows the long Bala fault which gave rise to the largest natural lake in Wales, via Dolgellau, whereas the Mawddach (or today the upper reaches of the Mawddach) rises in the mountains east of Trawsfynydd. The 'Maw' name possibly derives from 'Mawr' or 'big,' while perhaps 'Mawddach' comes from the mutated suffix 'bach' or 'little' attached to 'Maw.' If so, the meaning would be the 'Big-Little' river, a linguistic formation not unknown topographically, cf. Little Bighorn.

2. *Cheshire Observer*, 4 August 1894, p.8.

3. In English, Penmaenpool. Since Penmaen means 'Rocky head,' this location is distinguished – by its position above a wide stretch of the river – from Penmaenmawr in Caernarfonshire, 'mawr' being 'great/big.' In English of course 'pool' also serves the idea of 'port' which is appropriate as this was one of the Mawddach's quays, where quite substantial vessels were once built.

4. The memorial plaque spells the name as 'Perceval,' but his death was registered as Percival Gray. He was baptised in Oxford on 30 October 1873 with the name recorded also as Percival. His mother was Stephana Cartier Gray. She was possibly of French background and may have preferred the French spelling Perceval.

5. *Manchester Courier and Lancashire General Advertiser*, 3 August 1894, p.8.

6. *Manchester Times*, 10 August 1894, p.3.

7. The press reports speak of seven in the boat that went to Penmaenpwll, but from the names listed it is evident that there were eight: the two men, William Paton and Percival Gray, sisters Louisa and Margaret Ella Golightly, Sarah Greenwell, Alice Mallison and Edith Moore, who all died, and Ethel Packer who survived. Her testimony to the inquest initially omits Edith Moore from the list of passengers, but goes on to mention that she was steering. The newspapers repeat her error, hardly surprising for a young person giving evidence to a coroner's court less

than twenty-four hours after the accident in which her friends were drowned and she herself nearly died. The three (not four) from William Jones's boat who drowned were Marie Reid, John Newman and Herbert Woodworth.

8   *Manchester Times*, 10 August 1894, p.3. Charles Edward, evidently known as Edward, was born in 1864 at Belper, Derbyshire. His father was a maltster but his older siblings were acquiring jobs requiring a high level of literacy such as teacher and printer. He himself was employed as a merchant's clerk in 1891, lodging in Derby.

9   Meirionnydd Archives, Dolgellau, Z/DBK/2/531.

10   The weather that August was poor – cool and wet – though the Meteorological Office summary does not allocate any particular weather event to 1 August and makes no mention of the Welsh coast. It does refer to depressions as being 'rather numerous for the time of year,' with the prevailing winds being westerly, but 'The gales reported were few in number, and, as a rule, of very little strength.' It was only at the middle of the month, on the 14th and 15th, that gales were widely experienced, not at its outset, though of course local conditions can differ significantly, particularly on exposed coasts and estuaries.

11   *Yorkshire Evening Post*, 4 August 1894, p.3.

12   *The Poems of Thomas Love Peacock*, ed. Brimley Johnson, London, NY, 1906, p.330. Peacock (1785-1866) described Meirionnydd as 'the land of all that is beautiful in nature and all that is lovely in woman.' In 1811 he wrote, 'I am in high health and spirits. On the top of Cadair Idris I reflected how happy a man may be with a little money and a sane intellect, and reflected with astonishment and pity on the madness of the multitude.'

13   John Brown Paton, 'Public Libraries and the National Home Reading Union,' *Library Association Record*, (1908), 488-497, quoted in Robert Snape, 'The National Home Reading Union 1889-1930,' 2002, online and *Journal of Victorian Culture*, 2002, 7.i, pp.86-110. Born in 1831 in Galston, Ayrshire, where other Patons were butchers, John Brown Paton married a fellow Scot and settled first in Sheffield where his three elder children were born, then moved to Nottingham in the mid-1860s where he worked as a theological tutor. By 1881 he was recorded as 'Independent Minister and Principal of the Institute for training Ministers and Evangelists, MA Classics and MA Phil. London University.' The family lived at the Congregational College. His eldest son was already an undergraduate at Oxford, a scholar at Trinity College, who went on to Lincoln's Inn. At the 1891 census John was visiting his unmarried younger brother Andrew, a cotton merchant in West Derby, Liverpool. Back in Nottingham eleven students were in residence at the Congregational College he founded, looked after by

three additional domestic staff. In 1901 aged 70, he and his wife were visiting a widow in Sussex. Unusually they were listed before the head of the household, a mark of respect presumably. He may have preached widely. He died in 1911.

14 *Cambrian News*, 10 August 1894.

15 Rev. Davies was minister of Barmouth's grand Welsh Methodist (C.M.) Chapel, and Rev. Mather had been appointed in May as pastor of the English Congregational Chapel. He was renowned as a preacher, with published sermons. (*Cambrian News*, 19 May 1893, p.6.) Both played dominant parts in the town's social life.

16 Testimony of Mr. Fields, from London, reported in *Shields Daily Gazette*, 2 August 1894, p.3.

17 'Epworth Terrace & St. Tudwald's [sic] Church from Bridge, Barmouth.' Postcard posted in 1909. The bridge referred to is the footbridge over the railway. The Catholic church, St. Tudwal's, was not built until 1905.

18 National Archives, Kew, COPY 1/418/760. Copyright owner and author of work: Henry Martin Appleyard, Barmouth, Merionethshire. Form completed 21 November 1894. Registration stamp: 30 November 1894. Other records show he spelled his middle name 'Martyn.'

19 *Leeds Times*, 4 August 1894, p.7.

20 *Cheshire Observer*, 4 August 1894, p.8. Another press report said they were 'Oxford University Extension lecturers, and were acting as companion guides to the party,' but the first part may have been inaccurate as Percival Gray had not yet taken his degree. *London Daily News*, 4 August 1894, p.6. John Brown Paton, William's father, Principal of the Congregational College in Nottingham, was involved in London University's extension programme.

21 *Nuneaton Advertiser*, 11 August 1894, p.4.

22 Early reports say he was from Tenby, for unknown reasons, though his father was born in Monmouthshire.

23 *Wrexham Advertiser*, 11 August 1894, p.4.

24 Rev. T. A. Leonard's evidence to the inquest. *Cambrian News*, 10 August 1894, p.2. It was pointed out that at the quayside William Paton did not claim to be an Oxford rower himself but just drew attention to Percival Gray. Ethel Packer, however, testified that Paton too was skilled in handling a boat.

25 William was the fifth of six children.

26 *Grantham Journal*, 11 August 1894, p.7. William's age was curiously given as 33 when the death was registered, but the 1871 census shows him aged 3. His birth registration was in the third quarter of 1867. He does not seem to appear in the UK 1891 census, so perhaps was abroad.

27 *Ardrossan and Saltcoats Herald*, 10 August 1894, p.4, reporting the *Liverpool Daily Post*. A poetic tribute concludes the Scottish report.

28 Alfred Vaughan Paton, also a cotton broker, was six years older than William, and an Oxford graduate.

29 There are two UK places with this name, one in North Wales near Mold, but this is the one near Wallasey.

30 *Worcester Journal*, 18 August 1894; *Cheshire Observer*, 18 August 1894. The Death Duty Register records that his residence was West Kirby and his father was his executor.

31 The carpet industry was a major employer in Durham at this date.

32 *Shields Daily Gazette*, 3 August 1894, p.3.

33 *Ibid*. Retail businesses combining trade in groceries and drapery were quite common at the time and continued well into the twentieth century. In Dolgellau today (2018) a business founded in the nineteenth century and still a draper's is remembered as having two counters until c.1960, the grocer's on one side and draper's opposite.

34 *Manchester Courier and Lancashire General Advertiser*, 11 August 1894, p.15.

35 *Leeds Mercury*, 4 August 1894, p.10.

36 Her name was given as Mallinson, or Malinson, in some reports.

37 *Leeds Mercury*, 4 August 1894, p.10.

38 *Leeds Times*, 4 August 1894, p.7.

39 Curiously Maud and Marie were also recorded in 1881 as daughters of the Fletcher family, Thomas Fletcher being a Wholesale Druggist. All the Reid children had F. as a middle initial, and Marie was registered as Marie Fletcher Reid in 1877, though how they came to be recorded in two households on the same night is a mystery.

40 *Cheshire Observer*, 4 August 1894, p.8. The spelling Maude occurs in the census record but her birth record confirms it to be Maud. The press reports all have the sisters' surname as Read or Reed erroneously. The group also included a Mr. Read who survived.

41 *Leeds Mercury*, 4 August 1894, p.10.

42 Early accounts say he was from Hastings, but this was an error. It was Frederick Pryor, formerly of Dunmow, who was in the same boat but survived, who lived in Hastings (see next).

43 Frederic(k) C. Pryor(Prior) was born in Dunmow in 1870, a solicitor's clerk still living there in 1891 with his widowed mother Ann, the youngest of her eight children. His father Henry W. Pryor had been a tailor. At the time of the accident he was still a solicitor's clerk, working in Hastings, but by 1901 Frederick was manager of a butcher's in Paddington, London, married with two children. It seems he may have been in Hastings with an Essex-born relative Charles Pryor who was a butcher there in 1891, living alone as a widower.

44 *Chelmsford Chronicle*, 10 August 1894, p.6.

45 She is down as an art student in the 1891 census.

46 *Sheffield Evening Telegraph*, 6 August 1894, p.4.

Chapter II

1.   *Manchester Times*, 10 August 1894, p.3.
2.   Ibid.
3.   Welsh is recorded as his only language, but Lewis Edwards spoke English as well. However, it seems the inquest evidence was taken in English, including that of William Jones.
4.   This vessel was the *Jubilee*.
5.   He also denied the hat story and that any young lady changed boats, and praised the final conduct of Paton and Gray – but this last testimony was necessarily based on supposition.
6.   *Sheffield Daily Telegraph*, 6 August 1894, p.4.
7.   David Arthur Hughes, 38, b. Cardiganshire, was recorded in 1891 as a surgeon living on the waterfront by the harbour at 1 Glanaber (between Graigfach and Porkington Terrace), with his Australian-born wife, 3 children and 3 servants. Ten years earlier he and his young family were boarding with a farmer in Llanddwywe a few miles up the coast. He was recorded as a Member of the Royal College of Surgeons, not practising. Perhaps he had just come to the district. News reports of the accident say he was the Medical Officer of Health for the area. He stayed in Barmouth, moving next to the Corsygedol hotel with its 17 staff in 1901. He died aged 52 in 1904.
8.   In 1891 Hugh James Lloyd, 49, b. Dolgellau, was recorded as a General Practitioner living at Tynycoed, an imposing house on the High Street which was to house doctors well into the twentieth century. He lived with his Irish wife and five children, a cook and a housemaid, but also employed a surgeon's assistant, 22, and a nurse, 18, who lived on the premises. He was actually the senior doctor of the two but was perhaps listed second as he was not the first on the scene. Reports of four doctors probably included these assistants. The 1881 census showed him as a Licenciate of the Royal College of Physicians. Ten years earlier he had been a young GP in Dolgellau. Llanaber churchyard has a prominent memorial to him as "General Practitioner in Barmouth for 33 years" with a tall white angel bearing a wreath and the text "Mark the perfect man and behold the upright for the end of that man is peace." He died in 1902 at the age of sixty.
9.   *Shields Daily Gazette*, 2 August 1894, p.3.
10.   Hampshire-born Thomas William Best was a retired army officer of 50, now chief constable of Meirionnydd. He lived with his wife, born in New Brighton, Cheshire, and young family, plus a servant, at the Doluwcheogrhyd mansion overlooking the Mawddach between Llanelltyd and Dolgellau.
11.   It is possible she was Lewis Edwards' daughter Mary, 21, though Edwards is a common name in the area.

12 *Manchester Courier and Lancashire General Advertiser*, 3 August 1894, p.8.

13 Frederick Pryor contested this account: 'He did not agree... that the river looked dangerous when the party started out. It was not dangerous till they were coming back against the wind.' *Manchester Times*, 10 August 1894, p.3.

14 *Liverpool Mercury*, 6 August 1894, p.5.

15 *Derby Daily Telegraph*, 4 August 1894, p.2. Charles Edward Harrison had perhaps injured himself in walking up from Bontddu to the gold mine in the failing light. The track is stony and rough. He would presumably not have attempted it if he had been lame from the outset.

16 *Huddersfield Chronicle*, 11 August 1894.

17 *Manchester Courier and Lancashire General Advertiser*, 3 August 1894, p.8.

18 *Shields Daily Gazette*, 2 August 1894, p.3.

19 The Jelf family were long established at Caerdeon, the mansion above the spot. The Rev. William Edward Jelf (1811-1875), an academic, built St. Philip's church nearby in 1862 for English-language worship, particularly for the Oxford undergraduates who came for classics tuition. His wife Maria, an artist, was sister to its architect John Petit. In 1874 their son Edward Petit Jelf married Fanny Reveley of Brynygwin near Dolgellau, adding the name Reveley to his name by deed-poll in 1891 on taking over the Brynygwin estate (Great Western Railway Shareholders records, 3 July 1891.) Charles Darwin rented Caerdeon in the summer of 1867. From the 1870s it was taken over by the Holland family (Coflein). The boathouse was evidently still known locally as Mr Jelf's.

20 In the 1891 census Thomas Garnett, who lived by Barmouth harbour, was down as a 'Boat Proprietor,' with a son of 22 a 'Mariner' and one of 18 a 'Boatman.' It is not clear why his boat was below Caerdeon.

21 Evan Edwards, a joiner, 43, lived at 1 Graig Fach on the waterfront, between Anchor Cottage and Penlan.

22 *London Daily News*, 4 August 1894, p.6.

23 *Derby Daily Telegraph*, 4 August 1894, p.2.

24 Annie G. Packer, William's unmarried sister, had lived with his family when they were in Nottingham, where he was also Clerk to the School Board, and was recorded as housekeeper. It seems after their move to Leeds she ran a boarding house in Barmouth for a while, before returning in her retirement to live with her brother and his family. Ethel was the eldest child and the only girl, with a string of five brothers. At the 1891 census she was staying with former Nottingham neighbours with several daughters, the youngest being of similar age to Ethel.

25 *Leeds Mercury*, 4 August 1894, p.10.

26 *Manchester Times*, 10 August 1894, p.3.

27 Thomas Arthur Leonard (1864-1948) had enrolled in 1884 as a theological student at John B. Paton's Congregational College in Nottingham, and had then supported him in his NHRU initiative, taking part as holiday organiser. With Paton he went on to found the Co-operative Holidays Association in 1897. He later worked with John Lewis Paton, another of J. B. Paton's sons, organising holidays abroad to foster international understanding. Wikipedia.

28 *London Daily News*, 4 August 1894, p.6.

29 *Liverpool Mercury*, 7 August 1894, p.7, reporting a letter to the *Standard*.

30 *Cambrian News*, 10 August 1894, p.8.

31 *Ibid.*, p.10.

32 *Leeds Mercury*, 13 August 1898, p.6.

33 From Cassell's *Rivers of Great Britain*, 1901.

34 *Cambrian News*, 13 July 1900, p.8.

35 This entry implies that William had been a nonconformist, as the rector or curate would officiate in church and then sign the burial register for a member of the established church, while nonconformist ministers (whose chapels rarely had graveyards) usually held funeral services at the home and then at the graveside.

36 H.D. Rawnsley, *Ballads of Brave Deeds*, London: J.M. Dent, 1895, p.63. Caerdeon is on the north bank of the Mawddach not far from Barmouth. Diffwys is the mountain at the eastern end of the range on that bank. Cadair Idris, the long mountain flanking the Mawddach to its south, which had long drawn visitors to the area in search of the picturesque, is named as the chair (Cadair/Cader) of the mythical giant Idris.

37 *Cambrian News*, 10 August 1894, p.8. The passage, and indeed the whole supplement, is a powerful reminder of the quality of much local journalism in the past.

Chapter III

1 Its nineteenth-century development included several substantial stone buildings designed to look like castles.

2 H.V. Morton, *In Search of Wales*, London, 1932, p.157.

3 'The River Mawddach. Barmouth. Merionethshire.' Rock & Co., London (founded by William Frederick Rock, 1801-1890).

4 Robert Southey (1774-1843), *Madoc*, X.94, 1805. In 1801 Southey toured North Wales with Charles Watkin Williams Wynne.

5 The river flowed on both sides of Ynys y Brawd (Friar's Island, where the monks of Cymer Abbey, Llanelltyd, once grazed their animals) with dangerous currents until today's causeway was built in the 1970s.

6   'The Bridge and Cader Range. Barmouth.' Postcard from painting by Carleton Grant, 1891, posted in 1904.

7   Merfyn Wyn Tomos, *Dolgellau 3: Industry and Commerce*, Dolgellau Partnership / Nereus, Bala, 2018, p.66.

8   'Mawddach Estuary from Bontddu.' Postcard posted 1917.

9   The Halfway House, Bontddu, closed in 2018. The inn sign shows Barmouth bridge.

10   Hugh J. Owen, *The Treasures of the Mawddach*, Dolgellau, 1950, facing p.59.

11   The date on the surviving autograph copy. The ten-stanza poem was published posthumously in 1918. The 1970 edition adds below the title 'For the Visitors' Book at the Inn' (pp.64-65). 'Hopkins's drawing of himself, made on a visit to North Wales in August 1864, from a page cut out of his 1864 diary.' Used on front cover of W.H. Gardner and N.H. MacKenzie, eds., *The Poems of Gerard Manley Hopkins*, OUP, [1967], 1970, and noted p.xii.

12   From H.H. Milman, *Samor, Lord of the Bright City: An Heroic Poem*, Book VIII, London: John Murray, 1818.

Chapter IV

1   Douglas G. Hope, 'A Boating Disaster on the Mawddach Estuary in 1894,' *Journal of the Merioneth Historical and Record Society*, VIII.ii, 2019, 158-177, published as this work was in its final stages.

2   E. Rosalie Jones, *A History of Barmouth and its Vicinity*, Barmouth: John Evans and Nephew, 1909, pp.44-45. Her work of 236 pages published in 1909 had been a major prize winner at the 1907 Barmouth Eisteddfod, written when its author was only sixteen. Elvina Rosalie, the daughter of John Jones, schoolmaster and librarian, and his wife Amelia, had been baptised by the Rector of Llanaber, Barmouth's parish, on 7 February 1891. At the 1891 census taken on 5 April she was recorded as 3 months old.

3   By chance a further pleasure boat disaster happened a week later on 31 July off the Cornish coast, when a small motor boat, the *Darlwyne*, was lost with 31 lives, 8 of them children. The enquiry found it had no licence, was unseaworthy and lacked safety equipment. The wreck was located exactly 50 years later in 2016.

4   The Merchant Shipping Act 1894. Report of Court No.8041. – m.v. Prince of Wales (Unregistered). Cited: dolgellau.wales/places/penmaenpool-1966-report.php

5   *Cambrian News*, 4 September 1908, p.3.

6   *Cambrian News*, 18 November 1910, p.8.

7   J.A. Houston was an established artist who had built a strong reputation particularly for historical painting (the English Civil War was a favourite subject) and later for landscapes. Although his best-known work is in oil he was also a fine watercolourist. In the 1881 census he is down as 'Artist figure & landscape,' his twin talents very evident here.

8   Kinnear was staying at a grand London hotel at the time of the 1871 census, aged nineteen and described as a 'Land Owner,' and presumably by 1872 either visited Barmouth himself and met Houston there or met the artist in London. Whether the finished painting, presumably in oils, survives is not known. Houston may have made the drawing either in preparation for the painting or more probably afterwards as a personal record. He was certainly in Barmouth in 1875 (also written on the mount).

9   *Cambrian News*, 19 May 1871, p.5.

10   Wikipedia. His mother's name is incorrectly given as Harriet.

11   There is also a local hospital at Dolgellau which can treat minor cases.

12   The lord mayor as well as visiting the Birmingham monument above the town, laid a wreath of poppies at the war memorial in the park where a service had been held on the Somme centenary, and attended a service at St. David's Church on the harbour commemorating the Sailors' Institute.

13   E. Rosalie Jones, *op.cit.*, pp.47-48.

14   The name of the vessel which foundered on Sarn Badrig reef, also known as St. Patrick's Causeway, which projects a long way off Talybont just north of Barmouth, part-exposed at low tide, is not known. It is thought to have been a French ship which went down with its cargo of marble in the first decade of the 18th century (the latest coin found was minted in 1702), but the bell by which it has become known is embossed with the date of 1677. (Mark Redknap, Sian Rees, Alan Aberg, eds., *Wales and the Sea*, CBHC/RCAHMW and Y Lolfa, Talybont, Ceredigion, 2019, 158-9, 246.) Where such a valuable cargo of marble was due to be unloaded is unknown. For the vessel to be at all close inshore suggests it was seeking a Cardigan Bay harbour, possibly Pwllheli. Porthmadog, of course, did not exist at this date. Perhaps a Llŷn landowner had grand plans for his mansion. It has also been suggested that it may have been intended for St. Paul's in London. (bbc.co.uk/wales/archive/bbc-north-west-wales-barmouth-bronze-bell-shipwreck.pdf, accessed 17.1.2020). It is not the only protected wreck site near Barmouth. The wreck of the *Diamond*, an American vessel from the 1840s, also a casualty of Sarn Badrig, is likewise under protection. (Mark Redknap et al., *op.cit.*, pp.170-1, 284.)

15   The museum is manned by volunteers, as is the small but evocative Sailors' Institute nearby which has maritime memorabilia. Both are

free. The museum is open most afternoons in the summer and by advance request at other times. The ground floor of Tŷ Gwyn, built into the rock, which is thought to have been a secure warehouse for valuable cargo such as wine, houses a café open at all usual times.

16 Tudur in Welsh, pronounced 'Tidder.' Its most famous monarchs were, of course, Henry VIII and Elizabeth I.

18 *Collected Poems*, London: Heinemann, 1923, p.29. Masefield's work was immensely popular. The 1923 collected edition sold 80,000 copies. Welsh myth tells of Cantre'r Gwaelod, of the drowning of land and 'many a sunken town' by rising sea levels in Cardigan Bay, which the tree stumps revealed at low tide at Llanaber suggest may be history.

19 H.D. Rawnsley, 'A Walk to Llanaber,' from *Sonnets Round The Coast*, London, 1887. 'Great Turra' – Tyrrau Mawr, or Great Towers – is the sheer face of the western summit of Cadair Idris seen from Barmouth. Thomas Pennant, the eighteenth-century writer and traveller, described it as 'one of the points of Cader Idris, the highest rock I ever rode under.' Hebog (Hawk) is one of the mountains of Snowdonia near Cardigan Bay and close to the boundary between the historic counties of Meirionnydd and Caernarfonshire. It is visible from the Llanaber shore.

Aerial View of Barmouth and the Mawddach Estuary